Endorsements for

Resting On The Heart Of Christ

THE VOCATION AND SPIRITUALITY OF THE SEMINARY THEOLOGIAN

D1284888

"Very seldom does one think of the role of a seminary theologian as its own calling. Dr. James Keating, in a profound and moving theological reflection, scopes out the contours of just such a vocation. In doing so, he explains how the theological enterprise fosters holiness and where theological discipline and discovery turn into prayer. This is a very important work, a voice crying in the wilderness, but it is now being heard."

Most Rev. David Ricken
Bishop of Green Bay, Wisconsin

"This book should be required reading for all seminary professors. Deacon Keating offers a challenging vision of seminary formation in which the way we study and teach theology is transformed by intimacy with Christ. He invites us to open our classrooms to prayer and silence before the mysteries we teach. This integrative vision reorients seminary education toward the formation of mystical-pastoral priests who can guide a spiritually hungry laity to Christ."

John L. Gresham, PhD
Kenrick-Glennon Seminary, Paul VI Institute

"This book is a timely invitation to consider anew the charism of the seminary theologian. Keating presents a clear vision for seminary theologians: teach out of a living communion with the Eucharistic Lord and invite the seminarian to receive and encounter this same Lord in his studies. By meditating upon John's Gospel in elegant language, Dr. Keating calls upon seminary theologians and future priests alike to be as magnanimous as Jesus: 'Only great love can bring forth great knowledge' (K. Rahner)."

Father Emery A. De Gaal, PhD
Associate Professor, Department of Systematic Theology
University of St. Mary of the Lake, Mundelein Seminary

"Deacon Keating's book is a refreshing treatise for all who have been called to educate candidates for the priesthood. This book will be of great assistance for all desiring to grow in their mission as seminary theologians and formators."

Father David L. Toups, STD
USCCB Secretariat of Clergy, Consecrated Life and Vocations

Resting on the Heart of Christ

The Vocation and Spirituality of the Seminary Theologian

Deacon James Keating, PhD

The Institute for Priestly Formation
IPF Publications

NIHIL OBSTAT: Father Joseph C. Taphorn, JCL

IMPRIMATUR: † Most Reverend Elden F. Curtiss
                Archbishop of Omaha

THE INSTITUTE FOR PRIESTLY FORMATION
IPF PUBLICATIONS
2500 California Plaza
Omaha, Nebraska 68178
www.IPFpublications.com

Printed in the United States of America
ISBN-13: 978-0-9800455-6-7
ISBN-10: 0-9800455-6-8

Cover design by Timothy D. Boatright
Marketing Associates, U.S.A.
Tampa, Florida

The Institute for Priestly Formation
Mission Statement

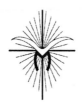

The Institute for Priestly Formation was founded to assist bishops in the spiritual formation of diocesan seminarians and priests in the Roman Catholic Church. The Institute responds to the need to foster spiritual formation as the integrating and governing principle of all aspects of priestly formation. Inspired by the biblical-evangelical spirituality of Ignatius Loyola, this spiritual formation has as its goal the cultivation of a deep interior communion with Christ; from such communion the priest shares in Christ's own pastoral charity. In carrying out its mission, the Institute directly serves diocesan seminarians and priests as well as those who are responsible for diocesan priestly formation.

THE INSTITUTE FOR PRIESTLY FORMATION
Creighton University
2500 California Plaza
Omaha, Nebraska 68178
www.creighton.edu/ipf
ipf@creighton.edu

Dedication

Bishop Felipe Estévez, STD, Auxiliary Bishop of Miami,
in gratitude for his support of and prayers for the mission of
The Institute for Priestly Formation

Father Dennis Billy, CSsR, ThD, STD,
Professor of Moral Theology
at St. Charles Seminary, Overbrook, PA, where he holds
The John Cardinal Krol Chair of Moral Theology,
in deep appreciation for his scholarship in the area of
integrating spirituality with theology.

Table of Contents

[Romano] Guardini depicts his arduous path to the doctorate and to academic professorship ... because German theology had submitted itself unreservedly to the methodological canon of the university, where only history and the natural sciences counted as science .... Guardini, in contrast, did not wish to become a historian or a scientist but a theologian.... Because he was conscious of doing something which was nevertheless entirely worthy of the university, he would say that *he was working for a university of the future which did not yet exist.* As far as I can see it still does not exist even today, but it ought to exist, and we ought to continue to work for it .... [One way of approaching theology] does not exhaust the whole of theology.

Joseph Cardinal Ratzinger
The Nature and Mission of Theology

Were Not Our Hearts Burning Within Us

The Second Vatican Council, in the Decree on Priestly Formation *Optatam Totius*, recognized that the renewal of the Church largely depended on the ministry of priests who serve the faithful. The council fathers declared "[T]he entire training of the students should be oriented to the formation of true shepherds of souls after the model of our Lord Jesus Christ, teacher, priest and shepherd."[1] Bishops, administrators, professors, spiritual directors, and pastoral formators must keep this goal in mind with the mission entrusted to them. The same council also taught clearly that the priest acts in the person of Christ the Head.[2] Thus through his spiritual, intellectual, human, and pastoral formation, the future priest must find his personal identity in Christ and Christ's relationship to the Father as beloved Son, who entered the world for the salvation of humanity. The future priest, like Christ, is sent into the world to lead the faithful to brotherhood with Christ, in the Holy Spirit, so that they may discover themselves to be the beloved children of the Father (1 Jn. 3:2).

In 1995 Archbishop J. Francis Stafford asked me to work with a group of priests to plan the founding of a new diocesan seminary in the Archdiocese of Denver. A religious order that had formed men for decades closed the seminary that year. The task was daunting, as my experience working in a seminary environment was limited to a short teaching appointment.

Archbishop Stafford was particularly interested in establishing a diocesan seminary similar to the seminary in Paris, especially with its unique spirituality year. After visiting the seminaries in Paris and Ars, and meeting with other rectors in the United States and Rome, I gained greater clarity on both the vision and the task. As planning continued for a diocesan seminary, Archbishop Stafford established a Redemptoris Mater Missionary Seminary in the archdiocese in March 1996.

While we had a wonderful building and excellent library in Denver, my greatest concern was bringing together a seminary faculty with the vision of the Paris seminary model and committed to the teaching found in the 1992 Apostolic Exhortation, *Pastores Dabo Vobis*, by Pope John Paul II. To add to the angst, Archbishop Stafford was called to Rome to serve as president of the Pontifical Council for the Laity in August 1996. He asked that I continue to work on the project as we awaited a new archbishop. Archbishop Charles Chaput was named Archbishop of Denver in March 1997. After his installation he decided to move ahead with the diocesan seminary project; he opened St. John Vianney Theological Seminary in the fall of 1999 and named me rector.

As a young priest I had read *Catechesi Tradendae*, the 1979 Apostolic Exhortation of John Paul II after the Synod of Bishops. It addressed the topic of catechesis and the teaching of Jesus Christ in our times. As Secretary for Catholic Education for the Archdiocese of Denver, I had used the document often; it spoke to my heart, especially when John Paul II descriptively wrote, "The definitive aim of catechesis is to put people not only in touch but in communion, in intimacy, with Jesus Christ: only He can lead us to the love of the Father in the Spirit and make us share in the life of the Holy Trinity."[3]

These words captured and expressed my own desire for every person entrusted with sharing the teaching mission of Jesus Christ and the Church. While searching for professors with terminal degrees to teach in a new seminary, I knew more importantly that I needed to find professors who desired to bring future priests into communion and intimacy with Jesus Christ. I wanted to find seminary theologians who not only were intellectually astute, strong communicators, and joy-filled, but also who were persons of deep faith and prayer, having a deep love for Christ and His Church. The separation that at times seemed to exist between academia and the spiritual life had to be bridged. In Paris I saw among the faculty that a unified theological life of both the mind and heart was indeed possible and real.

As you read Dr. James Keating's book, *Resting on the Heart of Christ*, you will discover the theological foundation for this bridge and unity. He provides, from both his personal experience and his extensive knowledge of theology, the important connection between theological rigor and the contemplative desire of the heart for union with the Trinity. He demonstrates that the seminary professor who is forming future priests is not only entrusted with providing men with the content of theology but also with leading them through their study to a deeper love of Christ. In this way the future priest will learn to exercise Christ's own pastoral charity in the world today and will be more capable of leading the faithful into intimacy with Christ.

Deacon Keating's research shows that this is not a new discovery but rather a recovery of the way theology was done in the past, especially by the Fathers of the Church. He provides testimony from the early Church Fathers as well as from recent theologians who have reflected on the truth of the relationship between an active, well-formed intellect and a heart that is in deep union with Christ. He notes that the most apt image of seminary theology today is one that sees the classroom as an extension of the Liturgy of the Word.

One gains this image with Christ on the road to Emmaus, in which He presents a lecture on salvation history to two of His disciples. Their eyes are then opened to recognize the risen Christ in the "breaking of the bread" and present in their midst. They reflect back on the presentation Christ gave to them on the road and state, "Were not our hearts burning within us?" (Lk. 24:32). The content of Christ's words given to them moved their hearts and minds to faith. *The discipline of theology should not only bring a deeper appreciation for new facts but also make one's heart burn with devotion in imitation of the love revealed in the heart of Christ. If only every seminarian after every class—be it Sacred Scripture, Church History, or Sacraments—could make such a statement as the two disciples! Jesus Christ is the model for the seminary professor!*

Dr. Keating provides abundant practical examples of how a seminary professor may use a contemplative model of teaching. The professor who follows the model offered will discover how to present the necessary material for the course of study while engaging the hearts of the seminarians entrusted to them. Thus the spiritual aspect of formation will truly become the integrative piece of the intellectual, human, and pastoral dimensions of formation as called for in the *Program of Priestly Formation.*

I encourage you to read this book prayerfully. Open your heart to the Holy Spirit, and quietly pray for the gifts of knowledge, understanding, counsel, and wisdom as you read. As a bishop, I pray that, as you read this book, the Holy Spirit will fill your mind and heart so that you may burn with a deeper desire to know and understand the wisdom revealed in Jesus Christ. St. Augustine reminded the faithful of his time, "Even now the Holy Spirit teaches the faithful in accordance with each one's spiritual capacity. And he sets their hearts aflame with greater desire ... as each one progresses in the charity that makes him love what he already knows and desire what he has yet to know."[4] For the seminary theologian especially, I pray that through your teaching you will help to form both the intellect and heart of the future priest; so that on the day of his ordination, as he is configured by the Holy Spirit to Christ the Head and Shepherd, he may have a heart after the heart of Christ.

Most Reverend Samuel J. Aquila
Bishop of Fargo

Notes

1   Vatican Council II, *Optatam Totius* 4, 1965.
2   Vatican Council II, *Presbyterorum Ordinis* 2, 1965.
3   John Paul II, *Catechesi Tradendae* 5, 1979.
4   St. Augustine, *In Ioannis Evangelium Tractatus* 97, 1; J. P. Migne,
ed., *Patrologia Latina*, vol. 35 (Paris: Garnier Press, 1877).

Acknowledgments

I would like to express my gratitude to Jessi Kary, AO, and Elizabeth Palmer, MDiv, for their generous work in editing this text.

I would also like to extend my thanks to Bishop Samuel Aquila of Fargo for writing the Foreword to this book. He is a true friend to *The Institute for Priestly Formation* and encourages all of us at IPF with his dedication to priestly formation.

Introduction

This is a book of spiritual reading. It is not a scholarly work on the nature of theology or on the history of the theologian. The aim of this book is to raise up in the seminary theologian's mind two realities for prayerful consideration. First, to be a theologian in a seminary setting is an office of great dignity and importance. Seminary theologians are not simply teachers in a prosaic sense but spiritual formators. We form men to become spiritual fathers, fathers who will sacrifice their lives for the welfare of the Spouse of Christ, the Church. Second, spirituality must assist the faculty in more effectively sustaining the mission of the seminary. The more seminary theologians are hospitable to Christ as they render doctrinal truth intelligible, the more they will be seen as true spiritual guides to the seminarians.[1]

This language is ideal, of course. As faculty members we desire to ensure that our influence is life-giving and selfless. For those reading this text who may have once held ideals but cracked them apart by their own immoral behavior or were the victims of other persons' behaviors, there is healing for you in Christ. He is waiting for you and desires to restore your peace and joy. Ideals are meant to inspire not depress. Despite our weaknesses and faults, most seminary theologians aspire only to sacrificial service in the name of the Church. As we deepen our love for our vocation in Christ through prayer and fidelity to our duties, our own happiness and virtue will draw the seminarians into a love for prayerful study and generous service to others. And so, can we deepen our desire to approach the teaching of theology in a way that encourages spiritual intimacy between ourselves and God and between the seminarian and God? Can we encourage one another to let Christ reach us in and through our professional activity and identity?

Intimacy can be an intimidating term. It can evoke images of sexuality or emotional closeness that is dangerous or imprudent. In this book I am speaking of intimacy with Christ through our study and research as seminary theologians. This intimacy begins in weakness before God and is born of our vulnerability before truth and the beauty of truth. Entering the soul at deep and abiding levels and converting our thinking and affections, this intimacy heals sinful affections and encourages us to be bold in word and deed. This boldness is not rash but tempered and ordered by our communion with the object of our study, the person of Christ. In this way the fruit of theological intimacy is commensurate with the gift of understanding. This understanding invites us to always hold in our memory the true nature of theological work, which is to yield holiness in the practitioner. When all is said and done, we are to be witnesses to the search for holiness. This is our gift to the seminarian. Theologians who surrender to the presence of Christ in their work invite the embrace of God, and in so doing they evoke the interest of the seminarian in a mystical-pastoral theology.

Study as a Personal Encounter with God

"Do not let study extinguish the spirit of prayer," St. Francis said to St. Anthony after giving Anthony permission to teach theology to the friars.[2] This medieval warning highlights the perennial tension between the *study* of the Word of God and a *personal encounter* with the Word of God as prayer. Critical theological method currently dominates university theology.[3] We need the fruits of the critical method, but there are hearts that have hungered for a more personal study of theology—and these hearts fill many of the seats in the classrooms of diocesan seminaries.

I taught theology at a seminary for thirteen years and became familiar with the cries of seminarians asking for a more integrated approach to studying theology, an approach that reverences both content and encounter. These seminarians knew that their future parishioners were interested in knowing Christ, not becoming professional theologians. These men thought more vocationally; they thought in pastoral-spiritual categories, not categories of critical and scientific method. These vocational categories of thought do not simply indicate a raw state that needs to be disciplined by critical method. Rather, these pastoral-spiritual ways of thinking indicate the presence of *inclinations* essential for a man to become a pastor: the love of the Lord and the desire to meet Him in study and ministry. Graduate study is difficult, but for the seminarian it ought not to be void of spiritual growth. Such growth has long been hallowed in the *processes* of study, subjugating the unruly ego, but spiritual growth can also be developed and encouraged in the *actual practices* of attending to theological *content*.

For some in the seminary world, and in university theology, any theological method that does not have objectivity, distance, and critique as its defining approach is not well received.[4] The model priest for some theologians is a man who simply reflects the theologian's own intellectual and methodological interests. For these academics, the pastor ought to model himself after a university professor by entertaining, encouraging, and allowing debate, critique, and dissent in parish settings. The professor will argue that if the priest models himself in this way he will be respecting his parishioners as "adults." In reality, if a priest were to model his ministry upon academia he would extend the influence of the university method of suspicion and critique into the parish setting. This understanding of an adult faith response is ideological. To have faith and to approach the Church *in faith* is not immature or untutored. It is intellectually and affectively mature to approach the teachings of the Church *in trust*, since these teachings have their origin in the truth and goodness of God. A seminarian certainly wants to understand the faith, but he does not have to suspend his belief to prove to the academy that he is serious about graduate study.

In response to this somewhat limited approach to theology, some seminarians have tapped into an ancient approach to teaching and learning theology akin to *lectio divina*. As Pope Benedict once noted, "The faithful expect only one thing from priests: that they be specialists in promoting the encounter between man and God. ... [The priest] is expected to be an expert in the spiritual life."[5] These seminarians want to encounter God in study so as to draw their parishioners into that same encounter. Such a seminarian longs to be the mystical-pastoral priest Benedict XVI describes. The question for seminary theologians is this: How can we serve this longing while also calling the seminarian into the ascetics of study?[6] These seminarians certainly want to utilize their intellects, but they want to do so in the service of understanding the truth of doctrine, not in the service of current political, economic, or cultural ideology (the *lingua franca* of university theology). To approach theology seeking spiritual growth, the seminarian accepts faith *as the measure of experience*, not cultural experience as the measure of faith. The norm of any seminary theology classroom is to have the intellect welcome and rest in the luminosity of doctrine.[7]

The vocation of the seminary theologian and the formation needs of seminarians are deeply intertwined. Ideally seminary theologians will one day have a formation process *of their own*. To attain a university degree in theology is not sufficient to train one in the work of seminary formation; such work invites a new kind of degree, one that is explicitly ordered toward the mission of forming future priests. Of course any theologian can competently pass on information about his or her chosen field of study, but the affectively and spiritually mature seminarian cries out for more. Even though he may chaff against study, he often does so because theology does not speak to his vocation: the love of the indwelling Spirit and a call to mission in the parish. Barring any vice present in their consternation, seminarians want to learn, but fundamentally they want to be *formed*, formed to be spiritual fathers.

Public Witness Flowing from Interior Prayer

By developing such a theology to assist in the formation of future priests, we can form priests who lead laity *to the heart of Christ*. We will only ignite the true vocation of the laity—transformers of culture—when we facilitate their own intimacy with Christ. It is this *intimacy* that calls them to action. Few are going to risk their own or their family's welfare to promote the social teachings of the Catholic Church simply because such a person is an upright or ethical citizen. In light of what they will suffer, such transformers of culture must be fueled by the desire for holiness. The well-formed mystical-pastoral priest will assist them in enflaming this desire.

Only the quest for holiness sustains us in suffering the truth. Short of that, most of us exist and make choices largely out of self-interest. A strictly scientific, analytic, or critical approach to the teaching of theology to seminarians will not respond to the call of the Second Vatican Council when it summoned the laity to be apostles:

> The apostolate of the Church ... and each of
> its members aims primarily at announcing
> to the world by word and action the message
> of Christ ... The principal means of bringing
> this about is the ministry of the word and of
> the sacraments. Committed in a special way
> to the clergy, it leaves room however for a
> highly important part for the laity, the part
> namely of "helping in the cause of truth" (3
> Jn. 8). It is in this sphere most of all that the
> lay apostolate and pastoral ministry complete
> one another.[8]

Only a mystical-pastoral priest can accompany the laity to
the core of Truth, who is Christ, and then encourage and
teach the laity to live the Truth, to live Christ, in the ordi-
nariness of their days, despite the costs. The culture will never
be transformed without such courage, a courage drawn from
real knowledge of Christ's love.

Recognizing that we live in a time when political
realities trump theological symbols, I must note that my
highlighting of the vocation of the priest as one who *forms*
the laity does not in any way degrade competent lay people
with theological and spiritual expertise. Any emotionally
healthy priest formed in sound Church theology will look
to such lay persons to assist him in the formation of lay
apostles.[9] This ought not to discount, however, the vital
and symbolic place held by the priest in the formation of all
Catholics; he is the parish spiritual father. Only a lay person
deficient in formation or infected with political ideology as
his or her primary symbol system would deny that Christ

has placed the priest in His stead and gifted this office with the potential to unite all members of the parish around the mystery of Christ's own presence.[10]

In the course of our ministry of teaching, we touch the many interlocking realities of priestly formation that directly form the seminarian in the Word of God. By virtue of such a formation, we affect countless lay people and their formation as well. To serve in the seminary is to participate in the formation of the whole Church. In forming the priest, we assist indirectly in forming the laity.[11] Both laity and clergy are crying out for an encounter with God, not simply discursive information about Him. As seminary theologians, we can and will respond to this cry within their hearts because of our special vocation.

Theology is personal and ought to remain so. Theology is not private. It is a profession, a mission, a competency both earned and given—but it is primarily a relationship, a relationship between the theologian and God and between the theologian and the Church. Amidst the standards, practices, and demands of accrediting agencies and deans, we progress in happiness and virtue only if we progress in intimacy with the Person who has riveted our intellect in faith, hope, and love. To this vocation and spirituality I now turn.

Notes

1 In 1993 a document was issued by the Congregation for Catholic Education entitled, "Directives Concerning the Preparation of Seminary Educators." This work highlighted the unique formation needs of all those in faculty positions at seminaries. It envisioned that someday a special institute would be established to serve the spiritual needs of seminary administrators and faculty (2, 3, 12, 76, 77). The "Directives" also highlighted that those called to teach within a seminary faculty should be true "masters of prayer" (27). In order to achieve this end, the document challenged the appropriate leaders to establish opportunities for ministering to the spiritual and vocational formation needs of the seminary faculty. The "Directives" call for "special spiritual preparation" to be made available to those who are entrusted with seminary work (48). Ultimately, when the goals of the "Directives" are fulfilled, those persons who are called to seminary teaching would be formed in the dignity and power of their office by way of spiritual training, perhaps even prior to doctoral studies (48). See chapter three below for more on this document.

2 See Faustino Ossanna, OFM Conv., "The Meaning of Theology in The Franciscan Order: Francis' Letter to Anthony," *Greyfriars Review*, 17:2 (2003): 130. "To the work of hands and mind [Francis] adds the work of the heart, which sees further, which acts out of love, which transforms reading and learning into a gift. The school becomes a classroom not only for knowledge, but for wisdom, for life. [Devotion and prayer] transforms the act of teaching and listening into a grace-filled sacrament."

3 "The Bible becomes an object which the professor has mastered and before which (like any scientist) he or she is neutral.... When we wonder why spiritual poverty and aridity dominate some of our seminaries ... it does not take long to realize that one of the main reasons is the *way* Scripture is being taught in them." Raniero Cantalamessa, *The Mystery of God's Word* (Minneapolis: Liturgical Press, 1994), 84-5.

4 "The intellect of a true Christian cannot resist [the love of God], whereas the attitude of a completely autonomous science of religion is that of self-conceit.... The attempt to be as objective as possible is a welcome component of self-examination from which no one is spared by a faith [seeking understanding]. The cool gaze of rigorous science thus becomes *a moment*, though *only a moment*, of the experiment of a life lived in faith." Adriaan Peperzak, *Reason in Faith* (New York: Paulist Press, 1999), 141.

5 Pope Benedict XVI, "Meeting with the Clergy" in the Cathedral of St. John in Warsaw, Poland (May 25, 2006).

6 There are, of course, men who seek priesthood from more secular motivations. It would be my hope that such men will find in a spiritually-imbued theology the occasion for their own conversions or the impetus to recognize that their vocation lies elsewhere.

7 There are legitimate questions to ask in theology, questions that may lead to the promotion of doctrine's development. There may arise a need to receive the truth of a doctrine at deeper levels. History proves that there does not need to be unanimity among theologians as a group for the Spirit to begin the development process. This process can begin within an individual theologian who possesses insight as well as courage, since he or she will need to withstand the suffering that comes from being a prophet. Of course one does not claim the title prophet; it is bestowed when the Magisterium confirms a theologian's idea and takes it up into universal doctrine. Until such confirmation, and despite the claims of colleagues, "prophetic" theologians are men and women who are simply promoting their own private ideas, which are more or less useful.

8 Paul VI, *Apostolicam Actuositatem* 6, 1965.

9 *Catechism of the Catholic Church* (CCC) 900, (Washington, DC: USCCB Publishing, 2000).

10 *CCC* 1548.

11 The laity also form the priest, a gift I will touch upon in the book.

Chapter One

Theology: Original Sources Influencing Current Streams

*"Breast of the Lord: Knowledge of God,
he who rests against it, a theologian he shall be."*

Evagrius
Ad Monachos

In order to bring the spiritual mission and identity of the seminary theologian into focus, I will compare this mission with that of the university theologian as it is currently practiced by many. These meditations will orient us to a deeper appropriation of the spiritual reality that lies at the core of seminary theology, as opposed to the more secular and "professional" goals that a large number of university professors aspire to fulfill.

Eusebius first gave the title of theologian to St. John the Evangelist. This title reflected John's capacity to communicate the true doctrine of Christ.[1] All theologians aspire to be true communicators, bridging the distance between what is received by them in prayerful study and what is shared with students. Since this "what" is also a "Who," the location of this "bridge"—the theologian—can suffer this reception very deeply. Augustine describes this freely received suffering as an *invasion of divine speech entering the soul* of the theologian.[2] Contemplative theologians, in turning to God, are not simply suffering the limits of their finite intellect when developing a class or writing a book but are suffering a progressively deeper indwelling of God. As Gabriel Marcel noted, "the deepest part of me is Another." Likewise, Hans Urs von Balthasar summarized all of metaphysics under the mystery of love.[3] Theologians long to have the core of their being vulnerable to the coming of God in Christ.

Communion between theologians and the God we study is wrought by the purification and suffering known personally in our own intellectual, moral, affective, and religious conversion. God wants to live within us so that we can put an affectively-imbued mind, molded by love, at the service of the formation of priests. Seminary theologians ought not to be "the last enlightenment rationalists"[4] but the first of a new generation of mystic thinkers, drawing intellectual acumen from personal participation in the Paschal Mystery. We are called to enter the ascetical life in the hope of yielding a purified heart because the purified heart sees the divine light: wisdom. The pure heart possesses us and orders our theological work toward its fulfillment in prayerful discourse on the truth of who Christ is. Pope Benedict XVI expresses this reality as follows: "Faith ...is an encounter with the living God ... But it is also a purifying force for reason itself. ... Faith liberates reason to do its work more effectively and to see its proper object more clearly."[5] Who are the predecessors of today's theologians? They are those men and women who became experts at receiving and suffering the arrival of a pure heart.

In the formation of the diocesan priest, the pure heart of the professor helps to order the theology he studies toward increasing pastoral desire. This desire is enflamed and then rationally ordered by a life of interiority in the context of sacramental worship. Seminary theology serves pastoral desire: It deepens it, purifies it, and orders it rightly in ways that respect the man's capacity to receive the truths of Christ. We learn much about the purification of the heart by adhering to what the ancients of the Church revealed about their own interior life.

Meditation

In what ways can I order my class lectures to enflame pastoral desire within the seminarian? How can this lecture's content give prayerful direction to the seminarians' pastoral ministry?

A true master researcher who also understood the reality of purity of heart was Sr. Juana Raasch, OSB. By contemplating her writings, we can become aware of how our own hearts might be formed in love and docility before the presence of Christ the Teacher. Raasch reminds us that Scripture admonishes against "vain" thoughts. Avoiding vain thinking is crucial if we are to remain in communion with God and steer clear of the dangers of isolation and pride. Vain thoughts lack the power of divine truth and arise from places in our heart foreign to divine intimacy. They develop out of an inordinate need to thrust our ego forward (perhaps out of fear or envy) and eschew the rapt listening to truth emblematic of the theologian. For seminary professors, such listening or obedience is not a constraint upon our minds but is its very liberation. We are obedient when we listen to the Lord in love—thus our thoughts can be purified of vanity.[6] From such purity arises fruitful creativity. To this point Raasch notes the following:

> [H]aving a heart towards God also refers to having a longing for God, an eagerness for knowledge of the Godhead and holy things, and a freedom from distracting preoccupations, which fills the heart with [reverence] for the Lord and thus with the Lord's actual indwelling presence. [This presence] confers spiritual enlightenment and understanding. "Cleave to the Lord" is the Shepherd's counsel to Hermes, "and you shall understand and perceive all things." Purification and knowledge work reciprocally; understanding comes only with purity of heart.[7]

Gavin D'Costa notes this power of purified reason as well: "Prayer guides theological study ... [B]y virtue of cohabitation with the living and triune God through prayer and all that it involves and the life of virtue, the theologian increases in love, and love is the lamp of knowledge."[8] This love is suffered in us during the course of our commitment to live in the presence of God. This commitment to live in the presence of God, becoming a lover of God through prayer, study, and virtue, clarifies our thinking around the realities of "holy things." In the pure of heart, the mind is open to and before God. Thus, in loving this God, the mind thinks out of what it loves, profoundly influencing its humility to be led by this same object of love into all truth. For the pure of heart, God is "seen" by the mind, not by the eyes—seen by and within the human capacity to receive meaning. The effect of allowing oneself to suffer the presence of God is the suppression of "vain conversation." The pure person is the one who meditates upon the Word of God and makes his or her way steadily toward union with the Father, Son, and Holy Spirit.

Therefore, the seminary theologian is one who is open to the purification of vain thoughts. This would mean that we discipline ourselves and allow the Spirit to assist us in discerning and purifying ideological, political, partisan, and superficial notions out of our theological lectures. The pure theologian offers the seminarian true food, rich with nutritional value, for his long journey ahead. As with all of Christian life, however, it is not sufficient to simply repudiate what is wrong; we must positively love what is correct and good. It is the loving of Christ's truth articulated in doctrine, theology, and in the lives of the saints that truly ignites the seminary professor's mind. As Theophan the Recluse advises, *"the mind must be concentrated in the heart."*[9]

For truth to have power, it must be spoken in love. Purity of heart "enables a man to be a spiritual father and to guide others with an apt word."[10] In a sense, we find our way to purity and humility by fasting from this passing age (Rom 12:1-2), not in the sense of being ignorant of its complex streams of thought and values, but in the sense that we have no communion with such things.[11] The mind is pure and the character is humble because the theologian ultimately seeks communion with Christ's ongoing presence in the Church: His Word, His Sacrament, His Way. To this truth we cling: We seek assistance through grace in discerning and appropriating His way. The theological lectures and writings we produce are gifts given out of this process of purification.

Meditation

What type of seminary community would promote such a formation in purity of heart? What models of seminary theology can we consider so as to deepen this vision of our vocation and internalize purity of heart even more personally?

Seminary Theologians, Critical Theology, and a Pure Heart

After the Council of Trent, the founders of seminaries, particularly in France, held the spiritual dispositions of their seminarians to be "paramount."[12] Following St. Charles Borromeo's initial commitment to post-Tridentine seminaries, history welcomes the "giants" in seminary formation during the seventeenth century and beyond: Pierre de Berulle, St. John Eudes, St. Phillip Neri, St. Vincent de Paul, Jean Jacques Olier. As we move into the nineteenth century, particularly in the United States, we hear more of a call for priests to be "educated gentlemen" and less of an emphasis on sanctity and spirituality.[13] The priesthood in the United States became "practical" and less "supernatural" during this time.[14] One commentator on seminary life, Rev. John Talbot Smith, wrote in 1896 that seminaries took the spiritual life of seminarians "too much for granted."[15] It was assumed that major seminarians knew the basics of the interior life when in fact they did not. Joseph White, in his historical study of seminaries, notes that as of 1910 in the United States, "the record of how well seminarians' spiritual qualities were developed is fragmentary at best."[16] Most of the spiritual life of seminarians consisted of private devotional commitment with spiritual direction and frequent participation at the Eucharist. The European seminary model emphasized the supernatural and the call to holiness of the priest, but the trend in the United States was to accent the pragmatic and the pastoral.[17] Was there any hint of the supernatural in the academic curriculum of the priest as "educated gentleman"?

The curriculum of the American seminary in the nineteenth and early twentieth centuries placed heavy emphasis on the study of moral theology. Eventually seminary reformers argued that biblical studies deserved first place: "[T]he seminarian's principal study should be Jesus

Christ.... Christ is first, man is second."[18] The textbook gained favor during this period (e.g., Adolphe Tanquerey), and bishops and seminary rectors increasingly desired their faculty to study for advanced degrees in Europe. A rising tension developed between seminary professors inclined to take a more critical approach in their research and teaching methodology and Roman leadership, who defined a more cautious approach to theological creativity (e.g., Pius X's *Pascendi Dominici Gregis*). The Vatican moved to monitor more closely progressive scholarship, and by the early years of the twentieth century the seminary came to be seen simply as a school of professional learning with little or no intellectual freedom or creativity.[19]

To some theologians today the seminary is still judged to be "only" a school of professional learning. Upon being hired as a seminary professor I remember one of my theological mentors advising me, "Be careful: once you get into seminary work, you will simply become a catechist." Of course, in his opinion, this was the worst that could happen to someone with a doctorate. This kind of judgment can happen, however, only if the terms *creativity* and *freedom* are restricted in their use. For some theologians, being "creative and free" simply means the uninhibited exercising of a "right" to dissent in the classroom and in publishing. The current atmosphere in higher education still tends to favor a model of theology that pits the theologian's right to free inquiry and speech against an "oppressive" Roman authority located in the pope and bishops.[20] While the university theologian ought to be accorded due freedom in research and teaching, especially at the graduate level, the diocesan seminary theologian's duty and joy is fulfilled by creatively and freely teaching in such a way that a seminarian can *first see the truths* of doctrine and their implications for pastoral formation.

For seminary theologians, professional development and education is paramount in our formation, but the disposition to be a critic of Church doctrine is less of a need than in university circles. Being convinced that Church doctrine bears truth—truth worthy of reflection and not simply criticism—it took me some time as a graduate student to believe that such convictions did not betray my theological vocation.[21] I recall a time right after completing my doctorate when I was standing next to a brilliant young theologian during the keynote address at the annual meeting of The Catholic Theological Society of America. The speech had something to do with politics and theology. He turned to me and said, "I hope I live long enough to hear one good keynote address in this society on the theology of Bonaventure." I had become so indoctrinated with what the Society was presenting as theology (themes on ecclesial politics, ethnic groups, animal rights, etc.) that I almost forgot that it was acceptable simply to think with and deeply explore the ideas of saints. Universities generally offer the critical model as the only method for doing "real" theology, influencing all students at some level. There is an arrogance on the part of some university theologians who hold their particular approach to theology as the only approach. Those who attend college, therefore, and learn from these professors become the only students who truly "get it." The seminary is looked upon as some unfortunate outpost inhabited by moderately competent theologians. The worst thing a university theologian could do would be to enter such an intellectual wasteland as the diocesan seminary.

Over time I realized that, despite being trained in a certain theological culture, it did not fully serve the new culture to which I was called: the seminary. In seminary the purposes of theology are to serve a deeper contemplation of the meaning of salvation as real and relevant to both pastoral and eternal life. Revelation is not simply a theme by which to explore political or cultural ideas. Obviously the revelation of Christ has great import upon the meaning of politics, family, and culture, but revelation itself is always ordered toward personal conversion, salvation, and communion with God in the concrete lives of parishioners. Unless the revelation is received by ordinary persons who worship in church, no social or political implications to *the faith* will even be raised by Catholics.

In my younger years I struggled with this tension of trying to be a *seminary* professor while also ensuring that I still pleased the university "powers that be." It was tiring. As I entered more deeply into the nature of seminary theology, however, I realized that being a theologian in a seminary was not like being one anywhere else. There really was a place for a more generous approach to theological method. The seminary taught me to think of theology in light of the persons in the pews. These believers were truly awaiting pastors who could lead them into holiness. This constituency, and their spiritual and intellectual needs, became my resting place. I wanted to think about how theology could be placed at the service of holiness—my own, the seminarians, and their future parishioners. This approach was not the pastoral theology that university professors dismissed as "lite," but rather a more substantive mystical approach that leaned upon the great sources of theology with the hope of introducing pastors to what John Henry Newman called "the saintly intellect."[22] This intellect is formed within a love of the Paschal Mystery and a personal desire for communion with the Trinity. It was, in the end, not a new endeavor for me or for theology.[23]

From the time I began graduate studies I was fascinated with how spirituality might interpenetrate with theology. Later I came to realize that what I was interested in was the work of trying to mend theology, since it had become torn from its moorings in faith, in communion with God, having become merely a course of study in history, politics, and sociology. I felt such grief upon finding theology so separated from faith, and I knew I was not alone in that.

Meditation

Do you feel any grief over the separation of formation in holiness from the study of theology? Do you have any memories of a professor who integrated these for you in the course of your own studies?

What I learned over the years of teaching in a seminary was that a theologian can aim to inculcate *the faith in the seminarian at deeper and deeper levels*, a faith that opens him up to truth and does not handicap him as a thinker. Ironically, the university theologian was not really interested in faith. Consumed by questions of power, politics, liberation movements, diversity trends, tolerance of new ideas, and so forth, university theology was not very interested in meditating upon the intellectual meaning of adhering to Christ in love. Understood as the apprehension of the love of God known in the mysteries of Christ and guarded and promoted by the Magisterium, faith was simply *tolerated* on university campuses. In some theologians there is a sense of faith, a sense of trust in the person of Christ, but it is not an institutional faith; it is a faith held more as an individualistic affection for Christ. While such theologians enjoy the teaching of "religious studies" on university campuses, they also feel at liberty to think *against* Church doctrine, and even to separate Christ from the Church. This is not the usual disposition of the seminary professor.

Beyond this, it is not correct to say that intellectual creativity belongs only to dissenting university theologians, as if they bravely labor in the field of prophetic utterances while the seminary professor only dispenses catechetical porridge to groups of passive twenty-first-century seminarians. Creativity in seminary theology is not simply identified with the right or even desire to dissent from received doctrine. It is a creativity of dialogue and discernment between the truth of doctrine and the new ideas emerging in culture. In my experience of teaching in both seminary and university ministry classes, I have noticed hardly any difference between the questions asked by seminarians and the questions asked by lay university students around contemporary disputed issues in morality and dogma. They both want to know why the Church teaches a doctrine so difficult to live and so rejected by a large portion of Church members. Therefore, a seminary professor *has to be creative in the way fidelity is applied*, articulated, reasoned, and prayed within pastoral concerns, or students will be ill-served.

What Unites Seminary Theologians?

We teach and study theology within seminaries from an explicit viewpoint *of faith*, but do we also consider and promote the study of theology from an explicit viewpoint *of love*? Such an approach would certainly render the whole faculty vulnerable to God and one another, but what would be the fruit of making a faculty's love for Christ public in the course of academic duties? This public demonstration of love is not a kind of sentimentalism that one "shares" in the context of class lectures but is rather like the kind of love that one possesses as a spouse. Such "academic" love would be akin to the task and gift of becoming one who always prays (1 Thes. 5:17). This does not mean that students or colleagues hear us in the hallways muttering to God about how much we love Him. To approach the study of God's revelation in prayerful love is to be always and everywhere *influenced by such love*, like a spouse who is defined by the internalized presence of his or her beloved.[24]

Yes, theologians need to embrace theological creativity, a creativity that flows from the love of God and doctrine as carrying not simply ideas to be engaged, critiqued, reconfigured, or even rejected, but a love of doctrine that *suffers the entrance of its truths into the affections and intellect.* In a sense the seminary theologian is called to endurance, called to develop *the strength to receive the truth of Christ in His Church, not simply reform it, or develop it.*[25]

By way of such love, we become vulnerable to a prayerful encounter within our study carrel or classroom. This prayerful encounter always carries truth, and it tutors the professor and class in the ways of prudence regarding the message it carries. There is no ideological monopoly on prayer. When Christ is welcomed, He brings truth. In such a politicized time as ours, we look to Christ to bring truth to purify the heart, to remove our affections for vain thoughts, as Juana Raasch reminded us.

University Theology

In 1931 Pius XI introduced uniform standards and degrees to the pontifical degree program, including the doctoral dissertation and all of its critical methodology.[26] Such critical theology, however, is contextualized within a piety that is founded upon doctrine.

> But remark, Venerable Brethren, the piety of which We speak is not that shallow and superficial piety which attracts but does not

nourish, is busy but does not sanctify. We mean that solid piety which is not dependent upon changing mood or feeling. It is based upon principles of sound doctrine; it is ruled by staunch convictions; and so it resists the assaults and the illusions of temptation. This piety should primarily be directed towards God our Father in Heaven; yet it should be extended also to the Mother of God.[27]

The Magisterium is not against critical theology; the papal office itself established norms for higher theological studies. It does have a perspective, however, that differs from a more "enlightened" or secular mode of doing theological research and teaching. The formation of the priest in higher studies is not an individualistic endeavor by a man committed to methodological criticism at the service of a politicized academic freedom. Rather, these higher studies are to promote a rigorous intellectual grasp of what the Church knows to be true.

But the portrait of the Catholic priest which We intend to exhibit to the world would be unfinished were We to omit another most important feature,—learning. This the Church requires of him; for the Catholic priest is set up as a "Master in Israel"; he has received from Jesus Christ the office and commission of teaching truth: "Teach ... all nations." He must teach the truth that heals and saves; and because of this teaching, like the Apostle of the Gentiles, he has a duty towards "the learned and the unlearned."[28]

From Pius XII in *Menti Nostrae*, we read:

> Finally, this industrious zeal must be illuminated by the light of wisdom and discipline and inflamed by the fire of charity. Whoever sets before himself his own sanctification and that of other people must be equipped with solid learning that comprises not only theology but also the results of modern science and discovery so that, like a good father, he may draw "from his storeroom things new and old" and make his ministry always more appreciated and fruitful.[29]

Further along in the same document we find:

> The masters of the spiritual life state that the study of the sacred sciences, provided they be imparted in the right way and according to correct systems, is a most efficacious help in preserving and nourishing the spirit of faith, checking the passions, and maintaining the soul united to God.[30]

The study of theology for the seminarian and seminary theologian is presented by the popes as a habit of life that may act as *a healing agent* and *an agent of conversion* (nourishes faith, checks the passions, maintains the soul's union with God). Theology is also presented as an agent of *sanctification* and the foundation of true *piety*.

Today seminary theologians are invited to be converted by the truth of doctrine in the context of their relationship with the bishop's pastoral governance. Some theologians are tender about calling theology "faith seeking understanding" *in the context of an ecclesial commitment.*[31] They instead think that theology is principally at the service of prophetic utterance, a model that first holds association with doctrine and ecclesial authority more lightly.[32] To have a theology simply beholden to the "guild" of theologians, however, is shortsighted. This shortsightedness was pointed out by moral theologian Norbert Rigali in the context of a discussion about the case of theologian Roger Haight, who was censured by the Congregation for the Doctrine of the Faith (CDF) in 2004 over statements that Haight made in his book, *Jesus: Symbol of God*, that were "contrary to the truths of divine and Catholic faith ... concerning the divinity of Christ."[33] After this decision by the CDF, the Catholic Theological Society of America issued a statement criticizing the Vatican for taking action against Haight and barring him from teaching Catholic theology. Rigali notes that today's theological debates are held in public. No longer can theologians be "silenced" and told to write only in obscure theological journals or disseminate their ideas only to colleagues at professional society meetings. The ideas of progressive theologians will find their way to the media, either by their own doing or by way of the reporting of others on the web, on blogs, on internet news, and the like. In this culture, Rigali concludes, the theological community cannot simply be left independent of the Church at large to correct and challenge its own members in some in-house fashion.

> [The Catholic Theological Society of America] fails to address adequately the problem of how the contemporary Church should respond to public controversial theological

claims about fundamental Christian beliefs.... No account is taken of the Magisterium's duty to see that the Church is provided with all necessary knowledge about Catholic doctrine. When a theologian publicly makes controversial theological claims ... the Church at large needs to be made aware of the controversial nature of those claims.... [The in-house] theological process of evaluation, clarification, correction, and, if necessary, rejection of public controversial theological claims needs always to be not merely a matter of mutual, internal correction among theologians.[34]

Some university theologians wish to have the Magisterium enter the theological campus only as a last resort. In this current climate wherein the speed of media communications is measured in minutes and seconds (not months or years), it would be remiss of the Magisterium to be silent on judging the work of influential theologians who publish books or essays containing doctrinal error. One may reasonably question the method utilized by the CDF to investigate theologians, but that they have a right and duty to officially speak out against ideas that undermine the faith is just as reasonable. Ideas have consequences; the Magisterium knows the power of ideas, and at times it must not simply join a theological debate but end it with a judgment. In this way the larger Church knows not only the ideas of certain theologians but authentic doctrine as well.

Some quadrants of university theology are not ready for, nor perhaps do such theologians feel the need to develop or welcome, a new overarching model that includes both a contemplative feature and a positive regard toward the Magisterium's role in guarding doctrine. In fact such a call would be received as oppressive to some faculties, as they appear to draw their orientation only from the political canons of diversity, tolerance, and prophetic witness. These sources of thought, however, may not be substantive enough to carry theology into the twenty-first century. A good description of where this prophetic-critical method may be heading is found in a rewording of Robert Imbelli's notation on the demise of neo-scholasticism. Like the prophetic-critical method, neo-scholasticism was, at one time, the leading theological method:

> For [forty years the prophetic-critical method] had provided an ... attractive intellectual articulation for [university theologians] but of a sort and on a scale that proved insufficient to the expanded vistas [needed to form men as priests].... It often exuded a marked antipathy to [ecclesial formation and sacred doctrine]. In the hands of its rote practitioners, it became the intramural tinkerings of a [vast majority of the members of the theological guild].[35]

In contrast to the prophetic-critical method of theology that "conforms to this age" (Rom. 12:1), diocesan seminary theology is free to explore lecture content and teaching models. Seminary theology is attached to doctrinal truth and the mind's effort to search such and surrender to its compelling beauty. Within this search is room for a spiritual approach to learning that—in this current age of "religious studies"—would not be welcome on many Catholic college campuses, since they have staked much of their mission on hospitality to the doctrines of various religions and none.[36] After observing forty years of a prophetic-critical theology that has restricted the university to predominantly one teaching, staffing, and research method (political and theological tolerance/hospitality), seminary theology can paradoxically find its *rest* in the *dynamism* and diversity of the mystical, ecclesial mind. This mind, while positively ordered toward the truth of doctrine, has a flexibility toward method that is alien to many university theologians.

For the seminary theologian, faith is expected to lead to communion with God in the Church: creating the mystical, ecclesial mind. For the university theologian, critique is expected to clarify any error lodged in the articulation of doctrine or perhaps in the doctrine itself. Seeing criticism as the defining way of doing theology has led many current university theologians to hold up as heroes those predecessors whose thinking was rejected by the Vatican over the last forty years.[37]

As Neo-scholasticism was transcended as *the* way of doing theology in the latter part of the twentieth century, so the university model of theological method needs to be reformed and made more generous in welcoming other approaches. This prophetic-critical model is only *one way* of doing theology; it may serve the purposes of some theological department aims, especially at the graduate and doctoral levels, but a diversity of methods ought to be welcomed at the university. Critique is vital to theology as it attempts to accurately uncover the meaning of a text, whether biblical, liturgical, moral, or mystical. In this sense a critical approach to the study of theology is helpful and necessary but incomplete. Making an analogy between Scriptural studies and theology in general, we can affirm the words of John Paul II:

> Nevertheless this study [historical critical method of biblical studies] is not enough. [Theology] must help the Christian people ... live in communion with God. To this end it is obviously necessary that the [theologian] perceive the divine word in the texts. He can do this only if his intellectual work is sustained by a vigorous spiritual life.... [In this way the theologian] is to ask for the love that alone enables one to understand the language of God, who is love. While engaged in the very work of [theology] one must remain in the presence of God as much as possible.[38]

John Paul also noted that biblical theologians, and implicitly all other theologians, need to remain faithful to Church teaching in their work because theology is not a work of individual curiosity but a reflection upon texts that have been entrusted to the Church.[39] What the theologian thinks about, uncovers, and articulates regarding the content of revelation and the natural law is all at the service of the Church's goal of preserving and deepening its "personal relationship with God."[40]

The diocesan seminary theologian is now poised to welcome more contemplative pedagogies and lead the way in experimenting with a more integrated approach to learning, teaching, and research.[41] Robert Imbelli noted that the mystic element in theology has atrophied; he wondered whether the *way forward* in theology—avoiding an exclusively prophetic-critical approach on the one hand and a rigidly orthodox/magisterial approach on the other—is actually accomplished by going *down* into the mystical. As Imbelli writes, "The theologian is not a detached observer or a dispassionate reporter upon the activities of others, in the manner of a practitioner of ... philosophy of religion; but personally participates in the faith being reflected upon."[42] This communion with the matter studied enables us not only to discursively know our subject matter but also to enter into communion with the One whose very self-revelation encompasses the object of study.

Who, then, are seminary theologians? We are men and women who eagerly think out of a love for God in the ecclesial service of intellectually forming seminarians, whose desires are being purified by contemplative study within a sacramental communal life. We also assist the seminarian in discerning the desires of his heart, so that he may more freely participate in the call to share in Christ's own pastoral charity. In contrast to the cramped prophetic-critical model practiced by many in university theology, the diocesan seminary theologian is *free* to hold the truth of doctrine in positive regard and to undertake the duties of teaching and research in explicit faith, energized and ordered by prayer. This characteristic approach to theology reflects the mission of the seminary, but each of us must personally discern how our professional duties might also become a forum for intimacy with God. University theology has its own mission and its own future to ponder.[43] The seminary theologian builds on a history of being sent by episcopal leadership to form a theological mind within priests so they can best serve the laity in their own journey to holiness. The seminary theologian, therefore, has a unique calling to assist the bishops in their office of conserving the Church in the truth of Christ. Jesus promised that the Paraclete (John 16:7, 13) would help the bishops accomplish this, and so the seminary theologian wants to cultivate *a living personal communion with the indwelling Holy Spirit*, the Advocate who assists us in staying faithful to the living preaching of Christ (John 14:16-17, 26; 15:26).

Meditation

What do you think about this description of the seminary theologian?

> *"We are men and women who eagerly think out of a love for God in the ecclesial service of intellectually forming seminarians, whose desires are being purified by contemplative study within a sacramental communal life. We also assist the seminarian in discerning the desires of his heart, so that he may more freely participate in the call to share in Christ's own pastoral charity."*

What aspects of your doctoral training prepared you for your call to seminary teaching? What aspects of your post-doctoral formation assist you now?

Notes

1 Rino Fisichella and Rene Latourelle, eds *Dictionary of Fundamental Theology*, ed. (New York: Crossroad, 2000), 1060.

2 R. R. Reno, "The Return of the Fathers," *First Things* 167 (November 2006): 18.

3 See David L. Schindler, ed., *Love Alone Is Credible: Hans Urs Von Balthasar As Interpreter of the Catholic Tradition* (Grand Rapids: Wm. B. Eerdmans Publishing, 2008). See also Hans Urs von Balthasar, "Movement Towards God," in *Explorations in Theology III: Creator Spirit* (San Francisco: Ignatius Press, 1993), 15ff, where he leads one to the insight that "being and love are co-extensive." He develops his meta-anthropological approach to metaphysics further in *Glory of the Lord*, vol. v (San Francisco: Ignatius Press, 1990).

4 Reno, "The Return of the Fathers," 16.

5 Pope Benedict XVI, *Deus Caritas Est* 28, 2005.

6 Juana Raasch, O.S.B. "The Monastic Concept of Purity of Heart and its Sources," *Studia monastica* 8:1 (1966): 15. The five-part series includes: *Studia monastica* 8:2 (1966): 184-213;
Studia monastica 10:1 (1968): 7-55;
Studia monastica 11:2 (1969): 269-314;
Studia monastica 12:1 (1970): 7-41.

7 Raasch, "The Monastic Concept of Purity of Heart and its Sources," 8:1: 33.

8 Gavin D'Costa, *Theology in the Public Square* (Oxford: Blackwell, 2005), 128.

9 See *The Art of Prayer: An Orthodox Anthology*, compiled by Igumen Chariton of Valamo (London: Faber and Faber, 1966), 165.

10 Raasch, "The Monastic Concept of Purity of Heart and its Sources," 8:1: 40, note 3.

11 "Gregory of Nazianzus meditates on the nature of theology [giving] priority to spiritual formation over the intellectual. Theology 'is not for all men, but only for those who have been tested and have found a sure footing in study, and, more importantly, have undergone, or at least are undergoing, purification of body and soul.'" Reno, "The Return of the Fathers," 19.

12 Joseph White, *The Diocesan Seminary in the United States* (Indiana: University of Notre Dame Press, 1989), 17. This book has ideological leanings (e.g., see where White calls an archbishop's loyalty to Rome a "bias," 261); it can, however, bear fruit in one's understanding of seminary development.

13 Ibid., 9-17, 218.

14 Ibid., 220.
15 Ibid., 223.
16 Ibid., 223, 227.
17 Ibid., 236-237.
18 Ibid., 242.
19 Ibid., 264.

20 In a visit to the United States in 2008, Pope Benedict XVI reaffirmed the legitimacy of academic freedom but not in the sense that many professors understand it. "In regard to faculty members at Catholic colleges and universities, I wish to reaffirm the great value of academic freedom. In virtue of this freedom you are called to search for the truth wherever careful analysis leads you. *Yet it is also the case that any appeal to the principle of academic freedom in order to justify positions that contradict the faith and the teaching of the church would obstruct or even betray the university's identity and mission; a mission at the heart of the Church's munus docendi and not somehow autonomous or independent of it.*" Benedict XVI, "Meeting with Catholic Educators," Catholic University of America (April 17, 2008).

21 It is common today to argue that the role of theology is to criticize the faith. Seminary theologians, however, need to assist men in intelligently embracing and living the faith. We question the faith so we can have a deeper grasp of its truth, not replace it with our own theories. The faith does not have to conform to our questions or answers ("Today we tend to make our weakness the new norm" [John Paul II, *Veritatis Splendor* 104, 1993.]). This is the road many of our university colleagues take, upending the faith of undergraduates before they even have a chance to internalize its truth. As Father John Neuhaus put it, "Can you imagine Aquinas or Balthasar inviting college sophomores to interrogate [meaning: challenge] doctrines that they only heard of yesterday" (*First Things* 166 [October 2006]: 72).

22 See James Keating, "Newman: Theologian of Prayer" *Downside Review* (January 2004, 122:426): 1-18. See also: Terrence Merrigan, *Clear Heads and Holy Hearts: The Religious and Theological Ideals of John Henry Newman* (Louvain: Peeters Press, 1991), 254.

23 Hans Urs Von Balthasar, *St. Therese of Lisieux* (New York: Sheed and Ward, 1954), 169. "Similarly ... she treats her doctrine as the heart of theology. The way she is pointing to is not one way among others, it is the only way. 'I know no other means of arriving at perfection save love.... The science of love ... oh I desire that science alone.... [L]ove is the sole treasure that I covet. Jesus condescends to show me the only way that leads to this divine furnace. It is the way of a small child abandoning itself without fear into its father's arms.'" Balthasar laments the separation of holiness from theology. There is

real reason to hope that someday the *formation of seminary theologians, that is future seminary professors,* will be a true formation in holiness, and not simply academic mastery of a course of studies.

24 Hans Urs Von Balthasar, *Love Alone* (New York: Herder and Herder, 1969), 89.

25 Seminary theologians are invited to contemplate the object of their study in many creative ways; here I will suggest just two. The seminary theologian can approach theology as one would behold an icon and *receive* its beauty, truth, and presence, and/or as one would engage other types of religious art wherein the beholder is *drawn into* the painting as participant. Either way is proper, and both ways may be used according to the matter being attended to by a mind that is centered in the heart. More on these methods will be explored in a later chapter on teaching. Regarding the phrase to "suffer" the coming of truth, I simply mean that when one becomes open to receiving the truth, ideology or bias is replaced by light and reality. To have held onto private constructs for many years and confuse them for reality will cause one to suffer when truth is finally welcomed. This intellectual conversion is also an affective conversion because we grow to love "our way" of thinking within the reality we construct. When the truth is brought to one by Christ, it is also a religious conversion and thus may be accompanied by tears of repentance and the necessity to receive the mercy of God. Such suffering is a necessary prelude to freedom.

26 White, *The Diocesan Seminary in the United States,* 277-278.

27 Pius XI, *Ad Catholici Sacerdotii* 39, 1935.

28 Ibid., 57.

29 Pius XII, *Menti Nostrae* 66, 1950.

30 Ibid., 89.

31 A rich conception of faith and reason is not found in isolating the theologian from the sources of revelation as "living." When faith-imbued professors seek understanding of what they believe, they do so seeing faith as a gift to reason. Faith tutors reason to desire understanding "it couldn't know it could seek." Lawrence Hemming et al., ed., *Redeeming Truth* (Indiana: University of Notre Dame Press, 2007), 17.

32 See D'Costa, *Theology in the Public Square,* chapter 2. See also Msgr. Charles Murphy, *Models of Priestly Formation* (New York: Crossroad Publishing Company, 2006), for an overview of different ways theological formation in diocesan seminaries has been approached in the past and currently.

33 Norbert Rigali, "Ecclesial Responsibilities of Theologians," *Horizons* 33:2 (Fall 2006): 301.

34 Ibid.

35 Patrick Carey and Earl Muller, ed., *Theological Education in the Catholic Tradition: Contemporary Challenges*. (New York: Crossroad Publishing Company, 1997), 223.

36 There is some evidence that certain theologians are now open to exploring spirituality as a guiding reality in theological teaching and research; however, such theologians may still be wary of placing this same research in an ecclesial and magisterial matrix. See Philip Sheldrake, "Spirituality and its Critical Methodology," in Bruce H. Lescher and Elizabeth Liebert, ed., *Exploring Christian Spirituality: Essays in Honor of Sandra M. Schneiders, IHM* (Mahwah, NJ: Paulist Press, 2006). Conversely, the newer Catholic colleges in the United States may be more hospitable to the authority of the Magisterium but cautious in allowing any mystical, spiritual approaches to teaching theology since they believe subjectivism may undermine the role of reason.

37 See Ray Schroth, review of *The Rule of Benedict: Pope Benedict XVI and His Battle with the Modern World*, by David Gibson, National Catholic Reporter (November 24, 2006). Schroth lists some of the theologians taken to task by the Vatican and prized by revisionist thinkers for their prophetic courage. As Cardinal Dulles noted, "Room must be made for responsible dissent in the church, but dissent must not be glorified as though church authorities were generally ignorant, self-serving, and narrow minded" (Avery Cardinal Dulles, *The Craft of Theology*, [New York: Crossroad Publishing Company, 1995], 14). Ironically, for some theologians who revere doctrinal orthodoxy, to invite spirituality into the study of theology is viewed as detrimental to a seminarian reaching his only and true end of scholarship: command of the classroom content. I hope some of these fears will be allayed as these meditations continue.

38 John Paul II, "Address," in The Pontifical Biblical Commission, "The Interpretation of the Bible in the Church (Vatican City State: Libreria Editrice Vaticana , 1993), 9-11.

39 See John Paul II, "Address," 9-11.

40 Ibid., 11.

41 Oddly enough these characteristics of teaching may be more welcomed in the social sciences or humanities than in some university theology classrooms. See the interesting account of classroom methodology by a political scientist, Jeanne Heffernan, "Integrating Heart, Mind and Soul," in John Dunaway, ed., *Gladly Learn, Gladly Teach* (Georgia: Mercer University Press, 2005), 112-124.

42 Robert Imbelli, "Theologians and Bishops," in Carey and Muller, ed., 225, 227.

43 Rigali, "Ecclesial Responsibilities of Theologians," raises a vital point for university theologians today who may be too simplistic in their habitual stance of warily viewing the Magisterium as disruptive of their academic mission. Part of the motivation by many parents to pay high tuitions to Catholic universities is the expectation that classroom theology will not undermine the faith but support it. Will Catholic parents continue to support private universities that have moved away from such an understanding of Catholic higher education?

Chapter Two

Identity: Resting on the Heart of Christ

Theology may be legitimately approached as a way toward intimate familiarity *with* God, rather than it being simply an academic discipline seeking to articulate ideas *about* God.[1] There have been movements in theology wherein reason (philosophy) is caught up in spirituality. These movements encourage reason to entertain the spiritual, to welcome intimacy with God, without fear that students will become "soft" in their thinking. Such fear is mitigated because intimacy with God disciplines the theologian and the seminarian to love the truth and know the truth and find ways to resist letting the ideological masquerade as truth. Furthermore, intimacy with God gives both the theologian and seminarian not only a head full of content but also a heart that adores the

Author of that content. In other words, intimacy with God can guide reason in healing any gulf between the abstract and the affective, between the objective and the personal tensions of study, research, and teaching.

This intimate familiarity with God should take ascendancy in today's seminaries, ordering their mission to foster and guide pastoral desire. The popular culture is in search of spirituality and the supernatural in ways both sane and troubling. If the Catholic priest is not formed as a spiritual leader, the faithful will go looking elsewhere for such leadership.[2] The seminarian must become a priest who can lead all to a sensible and sanctifying rest in authentically spiritual ways of living—ways that draw their life from the mystery of Christ. Such spiritual formation—a formation that has its affective and intellectual source in the mysteries of Christ's life, death, and resurrection—is not to be relegated simply to seminary spiritual directors. Without the presence of theologians involved in the life of the Spirit, interiority becomes reduced to the realm of the private, material only for the internal forum. This type of reductionist thinking endangers the seminarian's ability to utilize the fruits of interior living as nourishment for his pastoral charity. The study of doctrine can itself be an encounter with the Divine as much as any explicit prayer or counsel given in spiritual direction.

Unlike those who labor in the field of "religious studies," we labor with our eyes wide open, since the Mystery has been revealed. We are no longer outside of a secret. We are living *in the secret revealed (mystic)*. We are living in the Mystery (1 Cor. 2:6-16; Eph. 3; Col. 1). This Mystery encompasses us, names us, and defines the way we think. Theology is mystical if we accept that our faith gives us access to *the* Mystery: God has become human for our salvation. For Hans Urs von Balthasar, "mystic" means an experience of the divine that is not only notional but existential. It can also have a meaning that is less subjective and more objective; for example, it can mean revelation or the Eucharist. The Church Fathers understood the *mysterion* to be very objective: It is the economy of salvation revealed and formed in Christ and continuing in the Church.[3]

Should seminary professors study in a school of mysticism for a time, "a school which gives practical and theoretical directions for mystical experience under the guidance of those who have already had this experience"?[4] Such direction would orient the professor into his or her own participation in the Mystery of Christ in Word, Sacrament, and witness (sanctity). Balthasar further delineates how to enter the mystical life: "It is not the experience of union with God that represents the standard for perfection ... but obedience."[5] How do we prepare seminarians to obey theology, to listen intently to all that Christ reveals? This kind of obedience is an *eager readiness* to receive truth and *a deep desire* to appropriate the skills of discernment. As John Paul II noted in *Orientale Lumen*, "When a person is touched by the Word obedience is born, that is the listening which changes life."[6] Theologians should have formation in being touched by the Word so that an interior listening is born in them, a capacity to listen in a way that changes their lives and helps them change the lives of seminarians. As a fruit of this listening, and the necessary discernment that accompanies all obedience, theologians will teach in such a way that elicits desire for mystical experience, for divine intimacy. The theologian is specifically called to teach seminarians how to *participate in the mysteries* they will preside over and offer in the name of the people and Christ.

Such spiritual formation for theologians may take the form of explicitly designed retreats, or more radically it may require the initiation of new kinds of training programs for those aspiring to teach in seminaries. I am ahead of myself, though; whatever the form, no such opportunities exist today. In order to think more clearly about our own formation as seminary theologians, how might we come to understand our mission toward the seminarian?

It is vital that we encourage seminarians to *love* the Lord and be purified by the love of neighbor, otherwise they will not receive the content of theology as knowledge but only as information, thereby distorting the exchange between the content of theology, who is a Person, and the one receiving, who is a disciple.[7] Intimacy with Christ is not measured fully by the degree of affective intensity present; rather, purity of mind and soul is the real standard. This purity is born of a loving knowledge of Christ—a knowledge of Christ that sends one on mission, not a knowledge that simply nurtures and heals. Such knowledge does indeed console, but then it also restores, rectifies, and sends its recipients in grace to "go and do likewise" (Lk. 10:37).

In seminary theology we must not lose sight of the spiritual formation that inheres in the learning process. If such temporary blindness occurs, the seminary becomes all about academic content. As we want to avoid the reduction of seminary to academics, so we also want to avoid the other pole as well: a seminary held captive to the ego needs of the seminarians. The ideal seminary life strikes a balance between the objective and subjective poles: helping the seminarian see the "otherness" of God as he receives the revelation theology plumbs (objective pole), which is best accomplished in a concurrent process of human and spiritual maturation yielding a man made ready for self-donation (subjective pole).[8] In this tension we can recognize the contours of Christian mysticism, wherein one desires union with the God but does not fear self-extinction.[9] As an academic good, the objective reality of theology always has priority over the subjective reflection of student and professor, but never in a way that diminishes the seminarian's need to truly *receive* the truth *as well as* learn about it. A seminary will want to promote the study of theology as a privileged place of conversion. In the end, such theology begins in worship and ends in acts of love, mirroring the mystic supper of the Eucharist itself. One is in union with God when he or she loves God *in the mystery of Christ* but still knows that it is "*I*" who am so loved.

Meditation

How does your heart respond to the invitation to study in the school of mysticism for awhile? Can you recognize God's presence in either your attraction to such a reality or in your hesitancy to accept it? Would responding to such an invitation be helpful in your own approach to seminary teaching?

As theologians we, too, are recipients and not simply dispensers of doctrine. We stand in fellowship with those who have passed on the truth from generation to generation. We are in a living fellowship with our forebears. In preserving Tradition, we preserve a living fellowship around the Truth. The Person of Christ is handed down in the Tradition and discerned in current thinking, it is upon Him that we bear down our affectively-imbued intellects. When we teach the mystery in faith and truth, *Christ is still teaching* in and through us, and we are still encountering Him in that same teaching. Obviously not all that one teaches as a theologian is normative for the Church, but it certainly must bear truth. When seminary professors teach in faith, when we receive theological content in trust and abandon our ego-centricity in such receptivity, then Christ is teaching the truth through us and healing error in the seminarians' hearts and minds.

Seminary teaching is not to be patterned after a debating society, or a revolutionary's platform speech, or a populist search for truths no single tradition can hold; rather, it is a holy, fascinating dialogue between teacher and seminarian based upon objective truth in the context of a worshipping community. The classroom as an extension of the Liturgy of the Word is a most apt image for seminary theology, wherein revelation is encountered and integrated into pastoral-spiritual realities. In utilizing the label "postcritical" Avery Cardinal Dulles articulated one way for us to understand this type of theology.

> Postcritical theology ... begins with a prejudice in favor of the faith. Its fundamental attitude is a hermeneutic of trust, not suspicion.

> Its purpose is constructive, not destructive....
> Theology ... is a kind of inquiry that takes
> place from within a religious commitment....
> The proper task of theology ... [is] under-
> standing the faith.... The contents of faith are
> known not by merely detached observation
> but by indwelling or participation.... Theol-
> ogy is moreover an ecclesial discipline.[10]

In this context, any intellectual difficulty or question we have about a text or a doctrine is received in peace and entrusted to further study, research, and prayer in a manner that continues to serve the end of seminary theology: the *embrace* of divine teaching within the affectively-imbued mind of future priests,[11] an *embrace* that yields pastoral desire. We teach in the manner St. Francis enjoined upon Anthony when he bid him to satisfy the seminarians' desire for prayer *in and through* theological teaching. As Dulles argues, the contents of faith dwell lovingly within us. Our first instinct toward theology is trust, not suspicion. This trust is present because the content of faith is known or is becoming known as the most substantive nourishment for our minds. In our study we pray; we encounter. If we approach the study and teaching of theology with a heart open to prayer, we can invite the seminarian to better grasp such a prayerful center as the source of study and pastoral charity. The seminarians' pastoral activity ought to originate within a divine relation-ship, a relationship not "interrupted" by study but evermore deeply secured by its contemplative nature.

Academic Formation: Teaching to Guide to Truth

I am describing a contemplative approach to theology founded upon spirituality. By spirituality I mean a kind of life that is free enough to be led unambiguously by the Holy Spirit—the abiding presence of Christ teaching theologians and seminarians all things and guiding them to all truth (Jn. 14:16, 14:26, 16:13).[12] Such an approach to theology will order the seminarian toward God in his studies and ground his pastoral desire in the Paschal Mystery. From such an approach, the future pastor will learn the necessity of contemplation, of letting God lead him to receive divine love and truth. "Contemplation means ... joining with the Eucharistic community of the church in remembering Christ's [Paschal Mystery] and then entering personally into this [Mystery] to share in Christ's journey from death to life."[13] This core self-gift of Christ to the world is what the seminary theologian and the seminarian are invited to contemplate. We are called upon to allow this mystery to enter our souls and, in so doing, to come to assist others in doing the same. It could be argued that this task and gift of contemplation is the very reason a man is called to the seminary in the first place—to be formed into a mystical pastoral priest. As a pastor he will contemplate this mystery not as an end in itself or simply for his own growth in holiness but as a gift for his people. He knows that his presence among God's people is only as grace-filled as is *his attending to* the mystery of Christ, an attending he learned in worship *and* theology class.

Despite so much emphasis over the last forty years in seminary formation upon *pastoral realities* being the lodestar of priestly mission, we are witnessing an unprecedented decline in parishioners' participation in worship.[14] Placing the weight of priestly formation upon his pastoral office and all its concomitant competencies has failed to keep the laity vitally interested in divine worship and the formational realities that flow from such a mystery.[15] People are searching for a spiritual life, for a place to rest in Christ, but apparently are not finding it within a *pastoral approach* that concentrates upon a pragmatic accommodation to the times.

In Western culture, the spiritual itself has become synonymous with the experience of searching and is reduced to an endless succession of novel and fashionable means with seemingly no real end or goal. Seminary theology can help the laity rest in truth and faith if it orders seminarians not simply to critical appropriation of theology and models of pastoral presence, but to both of these within a renewed vulnerability to divine encounter. Future priests can then be heralds of such an encounter for a population that is looking for a spiritual home, a place of rest for their hearts. Priests formed by a contemplative theology can bring the laity's hearts home to the living mystery of Christ. Pastoral desire, then, comes to be understood as *the fruit of the seminarian's own intimacy with the mystery of Christ* as appropriated intellectually, affectively, and experientially.

The last forty years of focus upon pastoral realities in seminary formation has recently been expanded by the United States bishops to include a renewed emphasis upon spirituality. All seminary formation, as represented in its academic, human, and pastoral dimensions, *must be integrated with the heart and core of priestly education: spirituality.*[16]

Spirituality is to be understood as I noted above, as a life of yielding to the Holy Spirit. More concretely, spirituality means allowing the mystery of Christ's own self-offering to be *lived out* by way of a faith-filled formation of conscience, which informs the will to act in concert with such formation. Specifically, spiritual living for the seminarian entails becoming vulnerable to Christ by way of full entrance into the human, academic, and pastoral formation process anchored in and informed by the fruits and graces of the Eucharist. This mystic encounter is the center of seminary life, from which all other realities ought to flow and to which all formational realities ought to find their end and goal.

The pastoral is inert when separated from spirituality. Ministry must be open to the fire of Christ's love for His Church and the priest's participation in that fiery desire. Without such a spiritual foundation, pastoral ministry is in danger of being reduced to competencies measurable by clinical approaches to ministerial presence. In other words, the seminarian's standard for ministry becomes his clear *self*-knowledge bearing a presence of unconditional positive regard toward the parishioner. This model is too easily prone to psychological, sociological, and political reductionism. The new *Program of Priestly Formation* with its focus on spirituality as the integrating heart of seminary formation (n. 115) orders the competencies of seminarians toward serving parishioners in their call to holiness. The pastor invites parishioners into the fire of *Christ's* unconditional love, *not his own* unconditional positive regard.

Meditation

Seminary teaching is a holy, fascinating dialogue between teacher and seminarian based upon objective truth in the context of a worshippering community. The most apt image of seminary theology: the classroom is an extension of the Liturgy of the Word. How would you approach your teaching if you held this understanding in your heart daily? Would anything change in your method? Would anything deepen in the method you are already utilizing?

The seminarian formed in contemplative theology asks God to let him be gifted with the same disposition as John the Baptist: "He must increase, but I must decrease" (Jn. 3:30). This gift will be given when he studies Catholic doctrine as a way to a prayerful encounter with Christ Himself. The asceticism of seminary theology is not simply known in the rigor of academic discipline but in the yielding over of the ego to Christ. In this yielding the seminarian learns to give the Bride of Christ what Christ Himself ultimately wants him to give—a ministerial mediation of divine intimacy. In the end , of course, the priest's affective life is satisfied in healthy friendships with fellow clergy, family, and friends, and not by offering his own *persona* or charismatic personality to the parish.

This is not to imply that the human qualities of a priest do not aid in facilitating parishioners' communion with Christ—they do. The "fat relentless ego" and its ravenous needs simply should not lead any ministerial agenda. In reality the priest has only one thing to give: a share in Christ's desire to reconcile sinners to the Father. Seminary theology is to be ordered toward that divine desire; therefore, we must serve that end in our classrooms by: 1) leaving room for prayerful encounters as prompted by the Spirit, 2) allowing for periods of silent receptivity of truth, and 3) forming questions that guide seminarians to appropriate their vocation as servants of lay holiness.

Classroom Theology

If spirituality is the core or heart of all seminary formation, what does this mean for the classroom? It means we must allow, invite, and receive the work of the Holy Spirit in our class preparation, lectures, research, and publishing. Prayer belongs entirely to the rational part of the soul; indeed it is the preeminent and most authentic use of the intellect. Prayer is not simply a matter of feeling and certainly not one of sentimentality. This is not to say that prayer consists of a purely intellectual act in the modern sense of the word, for intellect is not identical with understanding "but is rather to be rendered by the core of [one's] being ... the inner man."[17] Prayer is a fulsome use of the intellect, a love imbued intellect.

There is no separation in seminary formation between contemplative and pastoral formation either. One and the same priest is called to live out of both realities, realities that fuel one another and are not opposed. Theology in the seminary classroom ought not to be indifferent to either prayer or the instilling of pastoral desire. There is no objective viewing post from which we look down upon spiritual realities and pastoral realities, judging them to be irrelevant to our labors. Rather, we toil to facilitate integration within the seminarian between the love of God and the love of parishioners, by way of a prayerful and mission-driven approach to classroom teaching. These two loves are not simply to form the background music of teaching but rise up to *constitute* the professor's own presence and skill in the classroom. From the theology professor, the seminarian receives a doctrine that yields to prayerful encounter and whose fruit serves the spiritual yearnings of the Bride of Christ.

In emphasizing openness to the Spirit in the midst of teaching I am not trying to return to some mythically pure time in the history of theology; Cardinal Dulles argued that a pre-critical time in theology never existed. By its nature theology is disciplined by a rigorous method that distinguishes between truth and illusion.[18] To be sure we cannot return to the patristic and medieval periods. Too much has been learned about the relative good of modern methods of research and teaching. It would be irresponsible to try to abstract a past way of approaching theology to only serve personal affective needs and not the needs of the contemporary Church. As a caution for us today, however, Dulles noted that only the subjective ideas of theologians were subject to criticism in the patristic and medieval ages, not the canonical sources themselves. The Word of God was a privileged source: to be received and pondered and, most powerfully, allowed to convert the intellect, will, and affect.

Eventually, by way of Bacon and Galileo, followed by Locke and Hume, all thought and even ecclesial doctrine was to become subject to verification through the medium of doubt and criticism. Post-critical thinkers such as Polanyi and Balthasar came to castigate these earlier intellectuals because of their bias in favor of doubt. The road to truth does not require believers in Christ to cloak themselves in suspicion in order to prove to modernity their neutrality before tradition. It is not tradition that biases a person to the truth but stubborn and unreflective ideology.[19] Since we still live in a time of doubt, a doubt that breeds skepticism, seminary theologians need to encourage seminarians to stand firm in the faith despite the relentless questioning and criticism posed by popular and political culture. To stand firm the mind must be nurtured by communion with Christ. "The contents of faith are known not by merely detached observation but by indwelling or participation, somewhat as we know our own body with its powers and weaknesses."[20]

Following Dulles, the seminary theologian will want to explicitly think, teach, and write in favor of the faith, adopting a hermeneutics not of suspicion but of trust.[21] Ideally, seminarians will come to understand *what* the Church believes by making room for the object of their study, God. It is Him who, by way of prayer, guides their scholarship.

The faith is *not undermined* when seminarians or professors carry questions into the theological forum. Some questioning seeks only to understand and affirm the Church's teachings. When a seminarian holds ecclesial teachings in his heart as true, his questions and the questions of his professors will not undermine faith but allow him to enter more deeply into it.[22] Within this amicable disposition, critical thinking toward, or analysis of, Church teaching is good. Analyzing such content is paradoxical, however, since the Truth is also a Person, the Christ. To analyze a person is to make the relationship impersonal. Of course, we do not confuse the *expression* of truth with Truth Himself. Instead, we stand before the divine Other yearning to receive the mystery of His being in wonder, obedience, humility, and awe. Further, theology is always an ecclesial discipline; it subsists in the Church because the Church is the primary bearer of faith.[23] Reiterating Dulles,

> Theology, then, is a methodological effort to articulate the truth implied in Christian *faith*.... The correct articulation of the meaning of Christian symbols is not a science learned out of books alone but rather *an art* acquired through familiarity by being at home [in the church].[24]

To be at home in the Church is to live within Her out of trust, to know Her truths as life-giving, Her fellowship as sustaining, and Her traditions and leadership as necessary to assist one toward deeper intimacy with Christ. Out of such a home an "artistic theology" appears, that facet of the discipline that welcomes contemplation and not simply argument, encourages silence as well as persuasive rhetoric, wants to fill the class with listening and not simply speaking, and seeks *to apply the truth pastorally and mystically* so that it does not remain impersonally universal. Dulles argues that artistic theology is not antithetical to science and its methods, but it certainly is not exhausted by such, just as in a healthy home the personality and gifts of a father do not replace the gifts and talents brought to the home by the mother and the children. No one method of teaching ought to dominate theology.

Worship and the Classroom

If seminary theology is both science and art, from what source should such a paradoxical reality flow, and from what source ought it find refreshment in times of dryness? Foundationally, seminary theology should flow from worship. The priest's mind and heart are to be formed by the truth about who the Church worships. Dulles cautions, "If theology is not to regress, it must retain its close bonds with prayer and worship."[25] In the eucharistic Liturgy we are at the source of *our knowledge* of the Word of God, His mystery of love revealed by His own life, death, and resurrection. Here all theology has its birth. Theologians who draw their theology from the mystery of the Eucharist will remain faithful to its truths even as they *attempt to convey a contemporary expression* (art) of this mystery. All such expression has authentic and lasting power only if it is born of the theologian's participation in ecclesial worship, that is, participation in the self-offering of Christ to the Father.

Are these bonds to prayer and worship to be forged by simply affirming the centrality of worship in seminary life, or can *theology itself* welcome the seminarian into the classroom *as worshipper*?[26] To welcome him within this identity, and not just as a student, reverences the truth that the seminarian has had his mind and heart formed by the Paschal Mystery. If the seminarian has internalized his formation in Christ through contemplation and prayer, he can *receive the wisdom of theology* and not simply data. Seminary theologians ought to consider this identity of the seminarian explicitly when preparing classes and doing research—the seminary theologian's audience consists of worshippers.

Distinguishing between the realities of worship and theology serves each of their proper ends, but to do so too strictly mars the nature of seminary. Seminary endeavors to form integrated men who love Christ always and receive him in both study and worship. Yes, we know the difference between being in chapel praying and being in class learning, but both forums coalesce *in the one man* who is being formed. In class no artificial separation between study and prayer ought to be imposed, and no artificial call to prayer ought to be conjured. In class, as an extension of the Liturgy of the Word, theologians and seminarians ought to be free *to pursue* Truth wherever He leads *and to receive Truth* whenever He chooses to alight upon the affectively-imbued intellect. Knowing and believing interpenetrate. Wonder, silence, contemplation, and gratitude are not foreign to a seminary classroom. Since faith is a kind of knowledge, to be led by faith into intimacy with the content of the intellect's object is not ancillary to class but grounds its very rationality.

Our current historical period invites us to reconsider how seminaries approach formation in pastoral work and theological thinking. Has our current approach attached itself to mostly secular theories of knowing and practice but remained mute on welcoming deeper mystical streams of thought? Since the time of Dionysius we have distinguished between the mystical and the rationally demonstrable.[27] Today, however, the bishops call for a closer association between the mystical and the rational in priestly formation.[28] By making the spiritual central to formation, the bishops compel seminary theologians to think about this question: *How does the work of the indwelling Spirit in your heart and in the heart of the Church relate to the work of reason alighting upon and analyzing theological truth?* Ultimately, truth must yield to love even as this truth encompasses love.

> So: does love trump reason? Yes and no: if truth is a transcendental, and love is the meaning of being, to say that love trumps reason is to say that truth trumps truth. And indeed it can and it should: a smaller truth must always yield its place to a greater, more encompassing truth. To refuse to yield in this case would in fact be itself irrational in a radical way. But if the comprehending truth is truly true, the smaller truth will invariably find itself, not supplanted, but surprisingly fulfilled. In the end, the absolute supremacy of love is precisely what makes reason ultimate because it is what allows reason to embrace the very totality that remains, even in the embrace, ever-greater than it.[29]

A "smaller truth," such as the contents of any given theology class, "must always yield to a greater, more encompassing truth": the Spirit coming personally to the student and professor in prayer to ignite or sustain a conversion.

Objectively the content of a class may be about a constitutive truth of doctrine such as the Trinity, but *only* when this truth is personally and affectively received does a student receive the greater truth of his own intellectual and spiritual conversion. Protecting and promoting intellectual and spiritual conversion constitutes the culture of a seminarian's formation.[30] Such conversions come about more readily in prayer, prayer that may come upon the seminarian in class because the professor is teaching truth. Objective truth, academic discursive knowledge, will *not* be lost to a praying student but *only driven deeper and possessed in a more integral and dynamic way.* In fact, in a prayerful reception of and a prayerful lecturing on theology, truth will be fulfilled![31]

Meditation

What is your experience in prayer when you meditate upon the U.S. bishops' stance that "since spiritual formation is the core that unifies the life of the priest, it stands at the heart of seminary life and is the center around which all other aspects [human, academic, pastoral] are integrated" (PPF, 115)? What hope arises in you when you read that spiritual formation is the heart of seminary life? Alternately, what fears or difficulties arise within you?

Notes

1 Yves Congar, *A History of Theology* (New York: Doubleday Publishing, 1968), 74-75.

2 "It would be wrong to think that ordinary Christians can be content with a shallow prayer that is unable to fill their whole life. Especially in the face of the many trials to which today's world subjects faith, they would be not only mediocre Christians but "Christians at risk." They would run the insidious risk of seeing their faith progressively undermined, and would perhaps end up succumbing to the allure of "substitutes", accepting alternative religious proposals and even indulging in far-fetched superstitions. It is therefore essential that *education in prayer* should become in some way a key-point of all pastoral planning." Pope John Paul II, *Novo Millennio Ineunte*, 34, 2001 (underline added).

3 Hans Urs von Balthasar, *Explorations in Theology*, vol. 4, *Spirit and Institution* (San Francisco: Ignatius Press, 1995), 311-312.

4 Ibid., 318.

5 Ibid., 326

6 Pope John Paul II, *Orientale Lumen* 9, 1995.

7 Balthasar, *Explorations,* 326; cf., 329.

8 Ibid., 333.

9 See Thomas Dailey, OSFS, "Seeing He Repents: Contemplative Consciousness and the Wisdom of Job," *American Benedictine Review* 461 (March 1995): 87.

10 Dulles, *Craft of Theology,* 7-8.

11 The term "affectively-imbued intellect" simply expresses the reality that cognition is influenced by what the affections adhere to in love. Objectivity in thinking is achieved by a deep appropriation of what one subjectively adheres to in love. Such love makes objective thinking compelling when the love itself is ordered toward objects of love that are worthy of our human dignity. If the object of one's love is decadent, then one's capacity to move beyond the ideological, idiosyncratic, and transient is imperiled. There is no place for one to *stand in objectivity*; there is only the work of purifying the desires that lead one to adhere to a good in love. In such purification, cognition itself ascends to a more trusted level of apprehending truth.

12 Gabriel Bunge, *Earthen Vessels: The Practice of Personal Prayer According to the Patristic Tradition* (San Francisco: Ignatius, 2002).

13 Kevin Mongrain, *The Systematic Thought of Hans Urs Von Balthasar* (New York: Crossroad, 2002), 67.

14 In a profile of America's Catholic population released in 2008, the Pew Forum calls attention to a demographic shift, with younger Catholics

less likely to remain active in the Church, while Hispanic immigrants replace many of the "cradle Catholics" who no longer practice the faith. "No other major faith in the U.S. has experienced greater net losses over the last few decades as a result of changes in religious affiliation than the Catholic Church," the Pew report notes. Citing the extensive "Religious Landscape Survey," the Pew Forum explains that "roughly one-third of those who were raised Catholic have left the church, and approximately one-in-ten American adults are former Catholics." Only 41 percent of self-identified adult Catholics attend Mass each week, the Pew study found; this is lowest among young adults, with just 30 percent of Catholics aged 18-29 attending Mass weekly (Pew Forum, Religious Landscapes Study, February 2008).

15 The pastoral approach to Catholic life is of course necessary but not sufficient. We want to embrace a way of offering the Good News that adapts itself to the needs of a concrete situation so that the Gospel does not lose its power to speak to men and women and move them. In some incarnations of the pastoral approach, however, pastoral simply meant receiving a person "where he was" and then offering information about doctrine or moral life so that he could then "follow his own conscience." This reduced pastoral formation to appeasing the "gods" of Western isolationism and individualism, thus locking the parishioner in his or her own ego deprived of the sacramental, ascetical, and spiritual formation that is vital for a true conversion to be suffered.

16 United States Conference of Catholic Bishops, *Program of Priestly Formation* (*PPF*), 5th ed. (Washington, DC: USCCB Publishing, 2006), 115.

17 Bunge, *Earthen Vessels,* 33.

18 Dulles, *Craft of Theology*, 3.

19 Ibid., 5.

20 Ibid., 8.

21 Ibid., 7.

22 Rino Fisichella, "Theology," in *Dictionary of Fundamental Theology*, ed. Rino Fisichella and Rene Latourelle (New York: Crossroad Publishing Company, 2000), 1064.

23 Dulles, *Craft of Theology*, 8.

24 Ibid. A sense of "being home" in the Church is relevant in university theology as well. With the welcoming of many Protestants and non-Christians into Catholic university student-bodies and staffs some faculty and administrators practice an errant form of hospitality—downplaying the very Catholic identity that establishes the schools existence in the first place. This was done in the name of hospitality, but what kind of guest demands that the

host negate his own family identity? What kind of host would acquiesce to such a request?

25 Ibid., 9.

26 "[T]he truly divine God is the God who has revealed himself as *logos* and, as *logos*, has acted and continues to act lovingly on our behalf. Certainly, love, as Saint Paul says, 'transcends' knowledge and is thereby capable of perceiving more than thought alone (cf. Eph. 3:19); nonetheless it continues to be love of the God who is *Logos*. Consequently, Christian worship is, again to quote Paul, λογικη λατρεία; worship in harmony with the eternal Word and with our reason (cf. Rom. 12:1)." Pope Benedict XVI, "Faith, Reason and the University: Memories and Reflections" (September 12, 2006).

27 Fisichella, *Dictionary of Fundamental Theology*, 1060.

28 *PPF* 115.

29 David C. Schindler, "Towards A Non-Possessive Concept of Knowledge: On the Relation Between Reason and Love in Aquinas and Balthasar," *Modern Theology* 22:4 (October 2006): 598-99.

30 "Pastoral study and action direct one *to an inner source, which the work of formation will take care to guard* and make good use of: This is the ever-deeper communion with the pastoral charity of Jesus, which, just as it was the principle and driving force of his salvific action, likewise, thanks to the outpouring of the Holy Spirit in the sacrament of orders, should constitute the principle and driving force of the priestly ministry. It is a question of a type of formation meant not only to ensure scientific, pastoral competence and practical skill, but also and especially a way of being in communion with the very sentiments and behavior of Christ the good shepherd: 'Have this mind among yourselves, which is yours in Christ Jesus' (Phil. 2:5)." (Pope John Paul II, *Pastores Dabo Vobis* (*PDV*) 57, 1992 [emphasis added]).

31 "Truth speaks to the individual in his or her entirety, inviting us to respond with our whole being. This optimistic vision is found in our Christian faith because such faith has been granted the vision of the *Logos*, God's creative Reason, which in the Incarnation, is revealed as Goodness itself. Far from being just a communication of factual data—"informative"—the loving truth of the Gospel is creative and life-changing—"performative" (cf. *Spe Salvi* 2). With confidence, Christian educators can liberate the young from the limits of positivism and awaken receptivity to the truth, to God and his goodness. In this way you will also help to form their conscience which, enriched by faith, opens a sure path to inner peace and to respect for others." (Benedict XVI, "Meeting with Catholic Educators," Catholic University of America, April 17, 2008).

Chapter Three

Study: Lectio and Research

Christ: the heart in which all treasures of knowledge are hidden.

Hugo Rahner and Karl Rahner
Prayers for Meditation

In 1993 the Congregation for Catholic Education issued a document, *Directives Concerning the Preparation of Seminary Educators*, highlighting the unique formation needs of those teaching and working in leadership positions at seminaries. The Congregation envisioned a special institute that would serve the spiritual needs of seminary administrators and faculty.[1] The *Directives* also invited seminary faculty to be true "masters of prayer."[2] In order to achieve this end, the Congregation challenged the appropriate leaders to establish opportunities to minister to the spiritual and formation needs of the seminary faculty. The *Directives* call for "special spiritual preparation" to be made available to those who are entrusted with seminary work. Ultimately, when the goals of the *Directives* are fulfilled, those called to seminary teaching will be formed in the dignity and power of their office by way of spiritual training, perhaps even prior to doctoral studies. At minimum, and in light of the fact that such a formation process does not yet exist in the United States, the Congregation hopes that those who are already members of a seminary faculty will seek to embrace their mission by receiving the Mysteries of Christ at ever-deepening levels of personal appropriation.[3]

No specific formation in becoming a seminary theologian exists in any Catholic, doctoral-granting university in North America. Nor am I familiar with any European program that specifically trains seminary professors. Presently, the norm appears to be that the theologian is appointed to and/or hired by a seminary and then begins to learn "on the job." For the priest faculty member, his own seminary formation enables him to appreciate its goals. For the lay member of the faculty, such an expectation is not warranted, and explicit orientation into the meaning and purposes of seminary is crucial. Even for the cleric, however, formal orientation to seminary *teaching* ought to be required. Being a seminarian at one time and being a seminary professor now are very different realities. Theologically, for both cleric and lay theologians, the prevailing presumption—incorrect as it is—is that a doctorate in theology is adequate preparation to teach in a seminary.

The seven or so Catholic institutions that grant doctorates in theology in North America do not have a seminary focus; they simply introduce the student to the academy and the reigning methods the professional league of theologians utilize in research and writing. Even fewer emphasize a program of pedagogy for these future professors, but this might be changing in some curricula. For the most part, however, any explicit formation in becoming a seminary theologian must be individually initiated and sustained. Knowledge of an academic field at a graduate level and openness to varied and *ad hoc* service to the seminary appears to be the standard used by seminary administrators to assess if a new faculty member is sufficiently trained.[4]

The *ideal formation process* would be doctoral or license programs that specialize in training seminary professionals. Perhaps the degree would be a general doctorate or license in systematic theology. The curriculum would cover all the theological and philosophical courses mandated by Vatican and episcopal standards of seminary education. The coursework, however, would be infused with both a contemplative openness to prayer and a regard for the teaching skills needed to raise pastoral desire within future seminary students. Thus the *critical approach* to learning would serve the *contemplative approach*, and the contemplative would nourish and order *pastoral ends*.[5] For those with advanced degrees already in hand, a certificate program could be established for their first year of seminary employment. Since outlining a whole curriculum for forming future seminary professors is the work of another time, I simply wish to now draw us into thinking about how our completed academic work can be augmented by a contemplative approach to teaching and study.

Approaching Our Own Study: Themes and Methods

It is a privilege to be on the faculty of a seminary, though cynics might say that such a comment is too romantic since seminary work has become drudgery for them. On bad days it can feel that way. Such a vocation may be particularly challenging for resident clergy theologians who live, eat, study, teach, and pray within the campus confines. It requires a great deal of common sense, good spiritual direction, deep prayer and friendships beyond the seminary to avoid becoming "institutionalized" by the habits engendered in such routine.

Beyond these potential difficulties, it remains a privilege to be on a seminary faculty because such work directly influences thousands of people who listen to the message of God's love in Christ, mediated by the priest. To be a formator of the men who will preach the Word of God to people hungry for its healing is a blessing that cannot be overlooked and a responsibility that might even make one a bit nervous. If, however, our *competencies are sound* and *expertly acquired*, then we have little to worry about because the Holy Spirit will order our students correctly despite our weaknesses. Our spiritual lives will be built upon and interwoven with our own love of study and adherence to academic rigor, welcoming the Spirit who will work in and through our competence, not despite it.[6]

An Eye on the Formation of the Laity

Assisting the People of God in their own call to holiness by providing for them competently trained priests[7]—
who not only know theology but also have found God
within such study—is one way the seminary theologian
serves the wider Church. Seminary theology must never be
priest-focused per se but always focused upon the *great gift the
priest gives to the laity*, a heart desiring to pastor them in and
to Christ. One of the main "texts" for us to ponder is the one
that keeps before us *the face of the parishioner*.

In the second paragraph of the Second Vatican
Council's document on priestly life is this truth: "Every single
member [of the Church] ought to reverence *Jesus in his heart*
and by the spirit of prophecy give testimony to Jesus."[8] This
is a guiding truth for seminarian formation. How do I assist
men called to priesthood in their mission to form the laity in
an interior life ordered toward love for God, a love that gives
birth to a prophetic witness in secular culture? If the seminary is truly the heart of the diocese,[9] then from its students
flows the hope of the sacraments, preaching, and leadership
that animates laity to change the culture in the light of faith
and morals. Of course touching this single chord of seminary formation, *teaching ordered toward lay formation*, does
not neglect the other notes and chords that will be played by
the whole body that comprises the *Program of Priestly Formation*; a chord well-played reverberates throughout the rest
of the instrument, ordering all other chords in their proper
harmony.

The seminary theologian is invited to regularly engage seminarians in all aspects of priestly formation: the

spiritual identity of the priest, the pastoral competencies he needs to possess, and the intellectual acumen he needs to preach, counsel, and teach well. Above all, however, the professor is to engage in a theological pedagogy that takes a man deep into the mystery of Christ. If this is accomplished, the future priest will be able to encourage his parishioners to let God's love grasp their minds and so worship Him who radiates Truth, Beauty, and Goodness.

Meditation on our true dignity as teachers in the context of the school's mission can be a source of great spiritual regeneration. This, along with regular spiritual direction, retreats, daily prayer and worship, and silent reading in a prayerful disposition assists in healing any depressed mood, cynicism, or tedium that might plague us during our daily routine of teaching, study, counseling, meetings, and administration. By remembering our mission, we help the seminarian remember his. "Priests exist and act in order to proclaim the Gospel to the world and to build up the Church in the name and Person of Christ the head and shepherd."[10] Professors are about the work of forming men in a vocation that exists for the sanctification of the laity. Nothing in the formation of priests lends itself to building up seminarians' egos, as if by responding to the call of Christ the young man becomes entitled to certain personal privileges. We do, however, need to build them up *in virtue*, so that they can continue their mission of edification even when they see little or no immediate fruit from their work. Like any good parent who becomes schooled in patience and intercessory prayer within the functions of forming a family, we promote the development of virtue within our students and actively pray for them. Consolations may come to such parents, but lasting joy will only be known to them in the mature years when they look upon their children and marvel in peace over the fruit they have born in living lives of virtue.

Meditation

What does the parishioner need to know about the love of God, and how best might the seminarians seated before me in class bring that love to parishes? How might I assist seminarians to enable a transformation of consciousness within lay people, assisting in their move from being citizens of this passing age (Rom 12:1-2) to becoming public Catholics?

Forming Spiritual Fathers

Seminarian formation is not a convoluted expression of ideas gleaned from accrediting agencies but is at heart the coaxing of a spouse and father out of a man. This fatherhood is not achieved by pop psychology gimmicks or developmental steps found in self-help programs. This fatherhood is born out of the suffering known in welcoming truth, severing affection for sin, and embracing the growing delight of contemplating the goodness of others as gifts from God. Somewhere in our study and teaching we are invited to meditate upon the spiritual meaning of fatherhood. Contemplation of this theme equips professors in the vital work of assisting in the affective maturation of the seminarian.

Formation intends to move a man from being a *taker* to being a *giver*, a source of life. If we prayerfully remember the identity of the priest, we will not forget the purpose of our teaching theology.

The professor is called to form men into priests who inspire the laity to begin an interior life. This interior life is based upon the reception of divine love, a love that once received, gives birth to a prophetic witness in secular culture. In my vocation as a father of elementary- and college-aged children, I am regularly impressed by their ability to act with virtue or at least behave with good manners in public. They attend to others' presence, at times express empathy and wonder, and act in charitable ways. As a father I can only marvel at their growth in the public expression of virtue. I am keen to consider these behaviors of my children because I love them, and in a real way my communion with them is my life. Such pondering gives me delight. Following this delight, peace rushes into my heart, giving rise to gratitude to God for children such as these. This consciousness happens naturally, in a moment and without a trace of a mystical ecstasy, even though its source is housed within my faith in the Father.

Can we lead the seminarian to such a consciousness regarding the spiritual formation he will give his parishioners? Before entering seminary or during the early stages of formation, the affectively healthy seminarian will mourn the loss of his biological fatherhood. From within such mourning, however, we can guide him into the unique kind of fatherhood Christ is sharing with him. It is not one where fatherly pride will lead the future priest to say, "That's my boy," but it will be a fatherhood in spirit. It is a fatherhood that gives him grateful pause when he remembers all that God has done through his faithful presence to parishioners. Spiritual fatherhood radiates out of the priest to fulfill the laity's need to have a guide lead them to the interior life, lead them to the place where change, conversion, and maturity in Christ is secured.

Such spiritual fatherhood is different from the familial fatherhood away from which Christ has called the seminarian. It is, nonetheless, a form of paternal communion. When it is appropriate to do so in our theology classes, can we illuminate this form of fatherhood and invite the seminarian to contemplate the beauty of his specific fatherly call? Encouraging the seminarian with such a meditation will assist him in integrating his vocation with the theological material presented to him in class. We thus assist him in incorporating his spiritual fatherhood into the very act of being academically formed in the Word of God and the doctrine that flows from the Word. To have his specific call explicitly related to theology will shape his view of theology as a "subject" perennially relevant to who Christ has called him to be.

> Leaving father and mother, the priest follows Jesus the good shepherd in an apostolic communion, in the service of the People of God. Celibacy, then, is to be welcomed and continually renewed with a free and loving decision as a priceless gift from God, as an incentive to pastoral charity, *as a singular sharing in God's fatherhood and in the fruitfulness of the Church.*[11]

If, as theologians, we hold in our minds and hearts both the People of God and the priestly identity of spiritual fatherhood, we will craft a theology that is nourishing to the seminarian's identity in Christ. By being faithful to the identity of the priest in the execution of classroom method, teaching content, and formational counsel, *we align our vocation very closely with the men's deepest desires* and, therefore, serve the end of the seminary and not simply our personal theological interest.

Meditation

In what ways can I keep the identity of the priest as chaste spouse and spiritual father before the hearts and minds of the seminarians as I lecture?

Methods: Books to Ponder

Beyond the reality of paying intellectual attention to *the mission* of the priest to the laity and the priest's spiritual fatherhood, our vocation as seminary theologians is deepened and oriented by the *books we study*. What theologian does not love books? By the study of theological books, we hope to glimpse the truth of who God is through His revelation in Christ. Since we love Christ and His Church, we wish to fill our minds with the beauty of salvation history, God's unconditional love for us, and our access to this mystery in the sacramental life. The mind, imbued with such love, fires desire, and thus we set off to know.[12] Books bring us to and help to focus this knowledge. In our careful, loving, critical reading of books, in which we embody a contemplative receptivity, the truths of theology become more firmly rooted in us, enabling us to know theology not simply as divine *data* but divine *encounter*. We wish to share this way of rooting theology in our hearts with the seminarians as well. Such a rooting for them, however, will not be directly ordered toward further doctoral research as it was for us as theologians, but rather it will root their pastoral desire in truth, truth that is personally engaged.

As was noted in chapter one, there are numerous ways to approach study and reading. Here I will utilize a model that approaches study in two ways: as monks from the east gazing upon an icon and as an Ignatian spiritual director inviting a retreatant into a scene of Christ's life and ministry. The iconic approach involves the will welcoming the beauty and truth of what is pondered and allowing these to abscond with the heart, letting the heart be taken. The Western approach, as known in Ignatian prayer, invites the theologian to enter the truth that attracts and draws the affections, opening the theologian to be moved by the same truth. At first glance, one model is more receptive (being taken) and one more active (entering), but each completes the other and necessarily fleshes out the study of theology in a contemplative manner. We want to study in such a way that the mystery of Christ becomes rooted in "a mind centered in the heart;" thus the discursive way of thinking rests upon and is hospitable to the truths carried by the affections of the heart. In striving to live this integrated way of study, we can show the way of contemplation to the seminarian.

Recognizing the popular fear, I acknowledge that seminary theologians are not Carthusian monks. We have pastoral hearts or we would not be teaching in the seminary. Nevertheless, we cannot forget our main approach to such teaching: a contemplative approach rooting the truth in the heart, welcoming a loving empathy toward the spiritual and material needs of parishioners.[13] Without such depth, a depth whose content conspires to form the seminarian within all four areas of seminary life (intellectual, spiritual, pastoral, and human), his future ministry will be threatened by shallow roots, becoming scorched in the burning heat of weary activism. The *Program of Priestly Formation* character-izes the life of the diocesan priest as one ordered by "steady prayer,"[14] possessing a "contemplative attitude [and] ... find-ing God in all things,"[15] resting on the fruit of an academic formation that enables him "to contemplate, share and com-municate the mysteries of faith with others."[16] Only through an appropriate contemplative formation (entered into dur-ing seminary formation and continuing after ordination) can a man sustain a lifetime interest in pastoral charity.

The Iconic Way

What does it mean to study theology in an iconic way? Icons are not simply illustrations or "art" in the usual sense, but aids to prayer and contemplation, windows to the

Divine. Our study of scripture, doctrine, hagiography, and more can be approached similarly: not simply as schoolwork but as aids to prayer. We study theology to *know God*, and we welcome the pastoral desire that flows from such learning; thus we can say that we do not read books "in the usual sense" but as aids to prayer and occasions for contemplation. Learning theology within this iconic stance bears fruit as a way to know God and be known by Him and as a way to usher the seminarian into a life of solitude, a life of "full" aloneness with God. Skills of solitude are urgently needed today. All of us are tempted to dash into the cultural rush, participating in event after event, resulting in feelings of emptiness when our activities inevitably end. The Western culture finds its meaning in *doing* many things. Only the man who enters a *communion of solitude* can carry meaning with him even when there is "nothing to do." Such solitary study not only benefits the theologian, but also assists the seminarian as a way to maintain meaning and communion with God in times of solitude—even to the point of eagerly welcoming such times, as a husband looks forward to being with his wife and children after a hectic, event-filled day.

Researching in an iconic vein can also begin to heal the theologian of minor neuroses or venial sin. Theologians can be competitive with one another, looking around to see who might be speaking more, publishing more, achieving more. In the university system, competition to catch the attention of colleagues and secure their approval for books, essays, tenure, and so forth is fierce. Since this is the air we breathe this competitive attitude may dictate our stance toward textual study. We may be compelled to read in order to articulate "that new idea" before anyone else does. We may be driven to read in order to refute the argument of that theologian who disagrees with our ideas either in print or in professional society meetings. In fact one might end up *always* reading, writing, and presenting with this rival in mind. Instead, iconic study is less about performance, measurement, and achievement and more about *being before the truths* of the texts and surrendering to them as a way to a deeper communion with God. Such study is not ordered exclusively toward endless engagement with professional colleagues. The fruit of such receptive deliberation may and perhaps *should be* published and reflected upon by others, but hopefully the attitude that governs contemplative study will assist in purifying any egocentric motivation. The asceticism known in this iconic study consists of receiving truths that aid the professor and seminarian *in their service to the Church*. Study is about service to the Church and Her needs, not my oftentimes misguided professional goals. Karl Rahner offered the following prayer about the kind of study he desired to attain:

> Be then the bread of my daily life. Be the deepest meaning of my study.... The tables of knowledge are richly spread for me. But they still leave me hungry. My understanding must busy itself with a thousand things to be learned. But often my heart remains cold and empty throughout.... Fashion my studies into the search for your truth which lies mysteriously hidden in all human knowledge. On the walls of my university stand the words, "The truth shall make you free." Let us never

overlook in our daily life that it was you who said this, you, the hidden Lord of all truth, the hidden king of all learning, the heart in which all treasures of knowledge are hidden. Only when I find YOU in all my quests for truth will I be free. Free from the narrowness of any one field of study, free from the desire for success, free from the greed of my heart. Only your kingly heart can teach me to love my study and knowledge, to put my best into it for your sake, to consecrate my heart in the service which I render to you alone in the depths of my love.... Only great love can bring forth great knowledge. Amen.[17]

As Rahner notes, Christ is "the heart in which all treasures of knowledge are hidden. Only when I find YOU in all my quests for truth will I be free." If we refer our study of revelation and our teaching about its contents to Christ Himself, then theology will become a way of perfection for us. It will be a way of identifying our sufferings in study and teaching with *the* way of Christ in the Paschal Mystery. Then our vocation will be a self-donation in the service of the holiness and virtue of the seminarian.[18]

In approaching the study of theology as we approach an icon, we possess a dispositional stance that is eager to let Christ find us, expectant of the Christ hidden in the text to draw us to Himself and not simply to some new idea. New ideas may indeed come, but they will carry theologians to rest in prayer and not merely in personal satisfaction. To "gaze" at the text does not entail some visual resting on the literal page, but a mental resting upon the truth when the love- and faith-imbued intellect is seized by the divine presence. In studying iconically, we are open to the asceticism of permitting a text to take us beyond the new idea, the affirming of the ego, or even the restless need to become *more* competent. Such study, rather, places our love of theology at the service of priestly formation. Guided by this service, we can expect an encounter with the Spirit of God in and through the truth apprehended by the mind, but also in and through the purification of our own character. To serve the seminarian as our goal does not reduce education to a crass notion of pragmatism or utilitarianism. No, we still delight in the truth known in the text, but we delight equally in seeing this truth integrated with the pastoral desire that defines the heart of the seminarian.

In iconography the image may represent more than the artist's offering to God, "but also God's descent into our midst, one of the forms in which is accomplished the meeting of God with man.... Thus through the icon, as through scripture, we not only learn about God, but we also know God."[19] The icon becomes a place of meeting, indicating God's desire to invite us to participate in His life. As we open our text to study, ponder, contemplate, and critique, we can mirror the iconic way as well. In a prayerful disposition, the texts we engage enter us as sacred texts, whether we are reading Scripture, the Patristics, or masters in our chosen field of study. As we rest in the text in faith, we rest in gratitude for the Spirit's leading us in and through *truth* to *intimacy* with God. The text captivates us, and while reverencing its objective truth, we ask the Spirit to reveal its relevance to the mission of seminary formation. We delight in being drawn into truth and develop it in our imagination so that such contemplation might better serve the seminarian.

Analogous to iconographers owning their unique approach to painting, seminary theologians ought to ponder their own approach to the art of teaching and research as well.

> The iconographic method of creating art consists of an asceticism wherein the artist ... consciously surmounts his or her "I," subjugating it to the revealed truth—the real authority of the iconographic tradition. The usual "I see it like that" or "I understand it like this" is entirely excluded in this case. The iconographer works not for himself, not for his own glory but for the glory of God.... The freedom of the iconographer consists not in untrammeled expression of his personality, of his "I," but in his liberation from all passions and lusts of the world and the flesh.[20]

Seminary theologians may argue that such a description of iconography can never describe theology. Perhaps so, but in a day when some university theologians promote and define their ideas as "prophesy" under the guise of a critical calling, it is refreshing when a theologian simply enters into teaching as an act of trust in the truth that is present in doctrine and worship.

Then-Cardinal Ratzinger observed something similar about the asceticism of the theologian: "The liberty of theology consists in its bond to the church."[21] Theology ought never to be afraid of or prevented from raising questions, but such questioning begins within established principles of the Church. Answers, doctrine, do not shackle the question but assist the teacher in ordering or even giving birth to better questions. The asceticism of the seminary theologian is not born of living within a sectarian enclosure but from living within an ecclesial-sacramental identity wherein the "I" gazes upon truth. The theologian is not unfettered, in a secular sense, but is in communion with the mystery revealed in and guarded by the Church.[22]

Jean Corbon is helpful in aiding our imagination about this iconographic model of seminary theology:

> The only obstacle is possessiveness, the focusing of our persons on the demands of our nature, and this is sin, for the quest of self breaks the relation with God. The asceticism that is essential to our divinization and that represents once again a synergy of grace consists in simply but resolutely turning every movement toward possessiveness into an offering. The epiclesis on the altar of the heart must be intense at these moments, so that the Holy Spirit may touch and consume our death and the sin that is death's sting.[23]

The theologian is called to turn "every movement toward possessiveness into an offering." In this way the work of theology becomes porous to the influence of prayer and objective truth, rendering it less likely that our own ideas will harden into an ideology. Reason has a new beginning in faith. The mind is taken up and made new in the encounter with Christ in prayer. *Now* conversion is the new foundation for thinking.[24] Thus, like an iconographer, the seminary theologian submits to the revelation entrusted to the Church, and enters this vast mystery hoping to bring light to the minds of seminarians through humility born of deep, personal engagement with the spiritual life.

> Let it not be said, therefore, that the theologian, as theologian, can reject revelation or that the Catholic theologian can reject the canonical scripture and dogmas of the church. To accept these things is not a limitation on theology but rather the charter of its existence and freedom to be itself.... The theologian seeks the intelligibility of revelation [and not simply the repetition of doctrine].[25]

As iconographers accept the "limitation" of ordering themselves to the Tradition without trace of ego, so seminary theologians place their intellect at the service of doctrine, preserving "the charter" of the theological vocation as well as personal freedom. St. Augustine declared:

> For teaching, of course, true eloquence consists, not in making people like what they disliked, nor in making them do what they shrank from, but in *making clear what was obscure*.... [I]t is one of the distinctive features of good intellects not to love words, but the truth in words. For of what service is a golden key, if it cannot open what we want it to open?[26]

In an iconic way of study and teaching, the seminary theologian is not primarily concerned with being current but with dwelling in the truth of Christ. Colleagues in secular universities may think that abiding within normative teaching is too restrictive. Lurking behind this criticism may be the fear that our freedom is diminished if we affiliate too closely with the Magisterium's conclusive teaching. *Normative* teaching, however, cannot be collapsed into *authoritarian* enslavement. We do not will to be taken *into authority*, a structure of ecclesial authority; rather, we will to enter the *content of truth* that such authority guards from this "passing age" (see Rom 12:1-2). Even the most creative revisionist theologians have normative content that defines their positions over and against current Church doctrine. Such theologians are being formed by these creative doctrines in the same way orthodox theologians are formed by abiding in the normative ecclesial teachings. We rest in foundational teaching or normative teaching because it is true, not simply because it is authoritative.[27] Further it is to be noted that passing on orthodox teaching to seminarians will not in itself secure a true and faithful priest—orthodoxy in the context of moral development and spiritual intimacy with Christ will secure such fidelity.

Ignatian Meditation

A second approach to study and teaching preparation considers our inquiries to be an Ignatian meditation—a meditation that paints a scene from Scripture and then bids us to enter and be affected by the love therein. At the beginning of each of Ignatius' Exercises, the retreatant takes a moment *to recall with reverence* all the graces God has given and desires *to give this privileged time of being with Him*. So it can be with us as we set out to study and prepare for class lectures. As the Exercises unfold, the participant is invited into the mystery of Christ's love, His power over sin, and His eventual triumph over sin and death in the resurrection. These are the very mysteries we ponder as theologians. In study and class preparation, we may want to borrow the Ignatian method of consciousness examen to facilitate a heightened awareness of how God is moving in our duties as theologian. Where is God drawing me closer to Himself in and through this study? Can I personally imagine my response to salvation, repulsion over sin, and joy over the resurrection?

We enter a personal engagement with the mysteries as we study them, not to convert the classroom into a time for testimony but rather to draw the seminarian into the splendor of doctrine. A student's interest in Christ will more likely ignite if our own theological study is fueled with passion for union with the One that our intellect is engaging. Many forms of media can pass on information; technology can inform (e.g., computer content), but only a theologian can share a living faith with the heart of a seminarian.

No matter how cynical and disenchanted experienced professors may become, due to personal suffering or affective pathologies, charity bids them to remember that the men sitting in their classrooms still believe that theology will lead them to know and love Christ. Any wounds that afflict our affect need to be given attention, so that we do not trample on the expectant love of theology, sometimes quite beautiful and pure, that seminarians hold as hope in their heart when they arrive for studies.[28]

Thus we are called to cherish this privileged time with God as we prepare to teach. Our consciousness of the Divine presence will be more or less apparent depending upon the circumstances of our day, the location of our study, the time we give it, and so on. To place theological study in the context of personal conversion does not infect the discipline of study with an agenda, but secures seminary theology to its proper end, the conversion of those who attend to its truths. Without such consciousness, the study of the Word of God may become mechanical, even drudgery, leaving the affect to order the will to repeat tired, old lectures (seen more in our own disposition toward the content than in the content itself), transmitting a perfunctory message to our students. There is no delusion here that any of us will always and everywhere be perfectly "on" when we teach, completely in touch with both the discursive truths and affective movements that arise in our hearts to tutor us. Approaching our class preparation in prayerful reverence, however, orders the lecture *from the beginning* toward a spiritual energy that we cannot will or gift to ourselves but which must be received from God.

Practically, Ignatian insight can lead us to approach lecture preparation in a way that enhances the lively faith our mind possesses. We can approach the study of the Trinity, Scripture, or the theology of sin and grace in a way that orients us to the reality and not simply to an instructional topic common to our discipline. As Ignatius bid his retreatants to place themselves in the unfolding mysteries of Christ's life, ministry, and exaltation, we place ourselves in the midst of the truth of our studies. We can begin our studies in silent expectation for a few minutes and at the conclusion receive the communion with God that truth carries.

Welcoming prayer that arises in the midst of our study is most vital. In remaining hospitable to prayer, the Spirit drives His beguiling truths more deeply into our being. Thus when we teach these same truths, the seminarians may know a taste of our experience. Again, this personal experience is not always something we make explicit. Rather, the Spirit makes it explicit within the heart of the seminarian in and through our communicating the truth. Such a transmission might end with the seminarian thinking, "All that I am studying is real." To receive such a grace is normal within a theology class. As theologians we have the privilege of facilitating this embrace of academics as grace. Rendering it any less compelling is a dangerous threat to the faith, hope, and pastoral charity of seminarians! The Spirit *wants* to lead us into all truth (Jn. 16:12-13).

Besides the limitations of our own character, intellect, and pedagogical skill, failing to generously meet the Lord in *our study* will render *our lecturing* even less compelling to the seminarian. Are we willing, in our study of theology, to enter the mysteries of Christ by way of conversation, as one would talk with a friend?[29] Setting theological study within an analogous relationship to the *Spiritual Exercises*, to meditation, are we ready to enter intimacy with Christ in deep trust, in rejoicing, rest, or even in repentance? Has the study of theology ever moved us to repentance? Has our study of our discipline ever led to a purification of our ego in light of the larger mission of the seminary or the formation needs of seminarians? Has our study ever led us to recant past errors in word or print or to heal past wounds with colleagues with whom we have disagreed in print or at the lectern? Can we study in a more contemplative way so as to receive the conversation that the indwelling Spirit is always having with us? Can we let this conversation affect us professionally?

In slowing down our study, in lingering over the text of our lecture notes or the research in which we are engaged, can we give the Holy Spirit a chance to catch our attention? Can we become more attentive in our interior life and catch the Spirit's movement within? Can we receive Him as He raises up the truth in a word, a description, or an argument, thus internalizing these truths as His presence? This movement by the Spirit, a movement of invitation to "come and see" (Jn. 2:38-39), allows us to be moved by what we study and ordered toward intellectual, spiritual, moral, or affective conversion. In the midst of our study, which can seem like a true ascetical commitment, are we "weak" enough to receive God from within the wisdom we long to understand and be defined by?

If we do not keep the *love* of God connected to the *knowledge* and *study* of God, seminarians will be tempted to separate the affect from the intellect, eventually leaving the Church with priests who seek enthusiasm instead of truth.[30] In an age when mystery has been banned from the university, and the reasoned appropriation of mystery has been banned from New Age retreat houses, the seminary must remain a free community that appropriates the Mystery as beautiful and draws the intellect into wonder and insight—producing wisdom in the priest.

Following the Ignatian way of inviting us into scenes of revelation that possess truth, they become conveyances of our own personal healing. Of late, I have come to appreciate one painting of a scriptural scene in particular, as a conveyance of truth, Ghirlandaio's *Last Supper*.

In this painting the artist has configured John, the Beloved Disciple, in a unique pose. Many renderings of the last supper depict John laying his head upon the shoulder or chest of Christ (Jn. 13:25), but in Ghirlandaio's expression, John's head is laying upon his own hands, which are placed on the table, as a young child might do during nap time in school. It appears to be a strange pose at first, until we enter the picture and realize that the artist has placed John's head, the central symbol of intellectual power, directly in front of the heart of Christ. Intellectual power was coming to the fore in a scientific, independent manner during the Renaissance (Ghirlandaio died in 1494, just as the high Renaissance was about to begin). In so placing John, the artist situates reason in communion with the Divine heart, the center and source of all unity between affection and truth. This painting then illuminates for the theologian the essence of devotion to the Sacred Heart of Jesus. In attending to this painting with our affectively-imbued intellect, we imaginatively rest upon the source of Christ's love of and obedience to the Father, His heart.

We need to listen to the heart of Christ so that the fruit of our listening can assist in sanctifying the seminarians in truth (cf. Jn. 17:17). Christ's rapt listening to His Father and the salvific mysteries flowing from this filial listening in love *is the truth.* Can we become free enough, through contemplating such truth, to enter a dialogue with God, a prayerful engagement in study and meditation? What is the source of that freedom? Could it be the gift of Christ's own freedom being lived in us, His power to listen deeply to the Father and enact in word and deed the fruit of His conversation? "No one comes to the Father except through Me" (Jn. 14:6). Christ, the God-Man, carries us into the Holy of Holies. The professor and student are to let their minds enter the heart of Christ and *rest in the truth He brings us to feast upon.*[31] In the matrix of sacramental living, theologians will know the coalescing of spirituality with academic theology in their own class preparation when they place the intellect before the sacred mysteries held in Christ's heart. In this manner of meditation and study one becomes a theologian:

"Breast of the Lord: Knowledge of God, he who rests against it, a theologian he shall be."[32]

This type of intellectual preparation is not solitary, individualistic prayer but, as the setting of Ghirlandaio's portrait suggests, deeply communal. Any fullness of listening to the heart of Christ happens at the "last supper," the Eucharist. From this environment of plenty, the encounter with the Divine Presence within the Church spills over into the work of the scholar's desk. Searching for the truth from within the intellect and surrendering to the grace of attending to the Lord in the Liturgy of the Word defines and orders the theologian toward a teaching method that also leads the seminarians back to that Word. *The classroom and the ambo are in communion*—but not to protect an endless circuit of academic and liturgical reflection yielding little or no pastoral relevance. The effects of such cooperative study between classroom and worship are known when the seminarian lays on the floor of the cathedral at his ordination and dies to all that is not of the Word. He is then "raised" with a mind penetrated by the mystery that led Christ to the cross of pastoral love and duty.

The breathing together of classroom and ambo is the same truth lived by St. John as depicted in the "Last Supper" of Ghirlandaio: The seminarian rests his intellect before the heart of Christ, not so that reason can be superseded by affect, but so that reason can illuminate the priestly mission of allowing Christ to live His mysteries over again in that same student. In this is the mark of the priest-scholar: a mind liberated to think with Christ out of love for what Christ loves, serving the needs of those who seek healing. This mystical-pastoral mind is one that wishes to be engaged in love, having no qualms about letting the beauty of what it knows lead it to offer its powers as a gift to the Church. "I no longer live, not I, but Christ lives in me" (Gal. 2:20). In this identity, this life's offering, there is enough intellectual content for many years of seminary formation. It is the privilege of the seminary theologian to shed light and clarity upon the truths that lead to so sublime an offering.

Meditation

In prayer, which method of teaching and study, the iconic or Ignatian, gives your imagination a new energy, a new direction toward which to order your current teaching and research? What other ways can you imagine teaching and studying that also invite you to a new level of contemplation?

New Designs for Priestly Formation

The seminary theologian is called to abide in contemplation. This contemplative approach to research and teaching serves to form men in priestly identity. Two models of such professorial formation were given above. There are, however, other approaches that may serve a seminarian's growth in interiority as well. The seminary has always been a place of tension between varying models and identities of the priest. The largest tension has arguably been between the monastic formation model and the formation needs of diocesan priests. To differentiate diocesan priestly mission from monastic spirituality, some thinkers highlight pastoral charity as the core identity and behavior of the diocesan priest; papal, conciliar, and episcopal documents also underscore this characteristic.[34] A commonly-held but misguided distinction (prone to descending into caricature) is that prayer is for monks and action is for diocesan priests. In truth the diocesan priest who fails to enact his pastoral activity out of a praying heart will soon be reduced to a social worker or counselor. No one expects the diocesan priest to become a Carthusian monk, but parishioners do want the diocesan priest to be prayerfully present to their needs out of the fruit *of his own intimate knowledge of Christ.* This charitable presence born of intimacy with Christ characterizes both the priest's interior life and his life of ministry. "The most perfect and enjoyable existence from a social point of view would be the most inhuman if it did not serve the interior life."[35] Furthermore, the interior life must be ordered toward pastoral charity; otherwise it can descend into a refined egoism.

To assist the theologian in forming priests who enact pastoral charity out of a praying heart, the current seminary culture will need to develop in new directions. "The essence of culture is the initiation into wholeness."[33] The promotion of the personal faith life of the seminary theologian is germane to the spiritual development of seminarians. For most seminary theologians, the idea of time for prayerful study is a fantasy presented by idealistic interlopers. Everyday seminary life is a round of teaching, committee meetings, faculty meetings, formation meetings (both faculty and with individual seminarians), and usually some administrative, part-time job either freely entered into to boost salary income (lay theologians) or taken on by resident priest faculty at the behest of the rector for the common good. Like the perennial cry of seminarians, the faculty can similarly chime in, "We have no time for prayer." For this cry to subside, a structural change within the seminary *horarium* must take place. Faculty members are overwhelmed with the amount of work that fills their plates—from involvement in seminary fund-raising efforts to teaching evening classes for the laity—and it negatively affects their mood and spirit. The whole argument of this book will go nowhere unless and until seminary theologians are given time, guidance, and material assistance to move their teaching method and preparation in a direction that welcomes contemplation.

Like any institution of higher education, the seminary has faculty who love research and publishing; some professors seek to study so as to add to the public theological conversation in journals and books. Likewise, some theologians prefer to focus mostly on teaching. The "publish or perish" threat has never taken root in the diocesan seminary. The absence of such externally imposed demands serves to relax some stress around performance. This is good. Relieving the publishing pressure on faculty is seen by rectors as a demand of charity. Even though there are many seminary professors who never publish books or essays, their classes still exhibit both depth of tradition and engagement with current ideas, thus becoming pedagogical models for others.

They may not publish, but they obviously do read and think. They are valuable assets to the institution.

The bottom line is this: How does the seminary *horarium* support or hinder these legitimate professorial roles? Whatever type of professor one is, all need time to study so as to appropriate, engage, and master theological content. More to the point of this book, they also need guidance in how to approach study and research as an occasion to be transformed by the Spirit. The fruit of such an approach is that contemplation and prayer come to define our stance toward the texts we are reading or writing. Such fruit, in turn, is given to the seminarian, who will normally receive it with great satisfaction and benefit. To be in the presence of such a competent contemplative is a reason the seminarian came into formation; to be in relationship with such a professor changes the seminarian for the better.

Any and all structural change must emerge from within the faculty itself, with the support and guidance of the rector. But even more must be imagined by the faculty: How is the Bishop, Director of Vocations, and laity involved in priestly formation? Minimum administrative standards for seminary formation must be met as codified by the *Program of Priestly Formation*, canon law, *Pastores Dabo Vobis*, relevant documents of the Second Vatican Council, guidelines of the Association of Theological Schools, and the oversight of accrediting agencies. These sources and bodies do not *apply* the codes, however; they *only mandate* what realities must appear in the seminary. The faculty and the rector apply the codes, and in such an application the seminary is free to explore what is in the best interest of that school.

The faculty and administration decide if they want to make spirituality the heart and core of diocesan seminary life. The more radical question is: Can such an approach be housed in our seminaries today, or do we need to develop new models? I think some new models are needed.

Some in seminary work will see my call for structural change as a dream to be dismissed. After all, they will argue, the parish priest is "run" by the duties and responsibilities within the parish structure. Why should the place of his formation be an oasis of prayer, when the rest of his life will be determined by the schedule of meetings imposed upon him by the real world? The prejudice in this argument is that ordering the seminary and parish from structures of prayer is somehow unreachable or maybe even detrimental—after all, we have real work to do.[36] I have never met an affectively and spiritually healthy priest who thinks that his "real work" is chairing meetings and feverishly moving from event to event throughout the day. Those priests who are happy within such structures "make it work" but do not think they were ordained for this kind of busyness. Husbands do not marry to cut the grass and paint bathrooms; they marry for the intimacy and friendship of a wife and children. Men do not become priests to chair finance and school board meetings but to share in the pastoral charity of Christ and preach the Gospel. All of the tasks in the seminary, parish, and family that "run our lives" need to be accomplished, but how, by whom, and how often? These tasks are not ends in themselves. Can we imagine a different kind of seminary producing a different kind of pastor?

Notes

1 Vatican Congregation for Catholic Education, "Directives Concerning the Preparation of Seminary Educators," *Origins* 23:32 (January 27, 1994): 2, 3, 12, 76, and 77.

2 Ibid., 27.

3 Ibid., 48.

4 There are some *post-appointment formation programs* sponsored by the Sulpicans, the National Catholic Education Association seminary division, and The Institute for Priestly Formation at Creighton University.

5 Pope Benedict XVI calls us to retain what is good in the critical approach to the study of theology while praying to develop a more generous appropriation of what reason encompasses. "[T]he act of faith is an event that expands the limits of individual reason ... and brings the isolated and fragmented individual intellect into the realm of Him who is the logos, the reason, and the reasonable ground of all being, all things, and all mankind." Joseph Ratzinger, "The Church and Scientific Theology," *Communio* 7 (1980): 339. See Pope Benedict XVI, "Faith, Reason and the University: Memories and Reflections" (September 12, 2006): "The courage to engage *the whole breadth of reason*, and not the denial of its grandeur—this is the program with which a theology grounded in Biblical faith enters into the debates of our time."

6 Such a trust in the power of the Holy Spirit, however, is not to be used as a rationalization for keeping emotionally or spiritually unfit teachers on the faculty. The wounds that such teachers inflict on seminarians are real and run deep. Such wounds are attested to in the healing work done by God, spiritual directors, and therapists, often years after seminary formation is complete.

7 The laity find and receive spiritual meaning by way of their work and vocation. It is also true that the priesthood is a gift to the laity in such formation by the identification of the vocation of priest with *Christ's will to continue His actions* throughout time and history in a sacramental way. To emphasize the dignity and the competencies of the priesthood in relation to the laity's spiritual lives is not a denigration of lay spirituality but its very foundation, a foundation built upon the sacramental life served by priests. This is a great gift. I have written about what *gift laity bring to priests* elsewhere; see James Keating, "The Priest as Spiritual Leader," *Origins* 35:10 (August 4, 2005): 176.

8 Vatican Council II, *Presbyterorum Ordinis* 2, 1965.

9 Paul VI, *Optatam Totius* 5, 1965.

10 *PDV* 15.

11 Ibid., 29.

12 "When the lover beholds the object of his love he is inflamed even more towards it. In this is truly found the ultimate perfection of the contemplative life, when the truth be not only known, but also loved" (Thomas Aquinas, *Summa Theologiae* II-II, q. 180, a. 7, ad. 1).

13 "He [Gregory the Great] tells us that the good pastor must be rooted in contemplation. Only in this way will he be able to take upon himself the needs of others and make them his own: '*per pietatis viscera in se infirmitatem caeterorum transferat.*' Saint Gregory speaks in this context of Saint Paul, who was borne aloft to the most exalted mysteries of God, and hence, having descended once more, he was able to become all things to all men (cf. 2 Cor. 12:2-4; 1 Cor. 9:22). He also points to the example of Moses, who entered the tabernacle time and again, remaining in dialogue with God, so that when he emerged he could be at the service of his people. 'Within [the tent] he is borne aloft through contemplation, while without he is completely engaged in helping those who suffer'" (Benedict XVI, *Deus Caritas Est* 7, 2005).

14 PPF 26

15 PPF 110.

16 PPF 26, 110, and 164, respectively.

17 Hugo Rahner and Karl Rahner, *Prayers for Meditation* (New York: Herder, 1962), 56-57.

18 See Robert Croken, et al., ed., *Collected Works of Bernard Lonergan* (Toronto: University of Toronto Press, 1996), 182.

19 V. Lossky and L. Ouspensky, *The Meaning of Icons* (New York: St. Vladimir's Press, 1983), 36.

20 Ibid., 42.

21 Joseph Cardinal Ratzinger, *The Nature and Mission of Theology* (San Francisco: Ignatius Press, 1995), 46.

22 Ibid., 18-27. See also Benedict XVI, "Meeting with Catholic Educators," Catholic University of America (April 17, 2008). "Teachers and administrators, whether in universities or schools, have the duty and privilege to ensure that students receive instruction in Catholic doctrine and practice. This requires that public witness to the way of Christ, as found in the Gospel and upheld by the Church's Magisterium, shapes all aspects of an institution's life, both inside and outside the classroom. Divergence from this vision weakens Catholic identity and, far from advancing freedom, inevitably leads to confusion, whether moral, intellectual or spiritual."

23 Jean Corbon, *The Wellspring of Worship* (San Francisco: Ignatius Press, 2005), 223.

24 Ratzinger, *The Nature and Mission of Theology*, 57.

25 Avery Dulles, *The Craft of Theology*, 168-169.

26 St. Augustine, On Christian Doctrine, Book 4, Chapter 11, art. 26.

27 Anthropologically we recognize that reason is wounded by sin. At times the appropriate way to overcome intellectual paralysis (compounded by personal sin and/or ideological prejudice) about a certain tenet might entail my giving assent to and entering the truth of ecclesial doctrine without intellectual clarity; entering by faith or action, my blindness over this truth may be healed. On rare occasions, appropriation of a doctrinal truth might have to occur by trust in the words of Christ alone that He has passed his own truth onto the Magisterium of the Church. I have seen this trust experientially affirmed for some people in the areas of sexual ethics, sacramental theology, and social ethics, wherein they were converted to truth once they began to live it in trust.

28 Obviously there are some seminarians that attend the theologate with wounds of their own, appearing listless before their studies and more interested in gossip, church politics, or currying favor than they do about meditating upon theology. In these situations it is hoped that spiritually and affectively healthy members of the formation team will notice and respond appropriately.

29 David L. Flemming, SJ, *Draw Me Into Your Friendship: The Spiritual Exercises* (St. Louis: The Institute of Jesuit Sources, 1996), 48.

30 Andrew Louth, *Discerning the Mystery* (Oxford: Clarendon Press, 1983), 6. A doctoral dissertation on Dietrich Von Hildebrand's conception of affectivity has appeared by Father Adam Hertzfeld, in which he makes the following salient points on the seminary theologian's approach to teaching: "The mind can know much more about God when it is enlightened through supernatural means—in other words, when it is enlightened by divine revelation, the fullness of which comes through Jesus Christ. It is this knowledge that truly puts a "face" to God and allows for a personal relationship with him.... With respect to the heart and the intellect it is clear that the intellect provides the heart with the intentional object to which the heart responds. This is a knowledge which is not merely conceptual but also personal. If the intellect were not involved in this process, the heart could give no response whatsoever to God because of the lack of any motivating object. With respect to God, the knowledge provided by the intellect comes from both natural and supernatural sources. It is the intellect which determines from an objective point of view whether or not the response of the heart to the object is appropriate or inappropriate.... Certainly, for von Hildebrand the heart gives religious conversion its fullness. Whereas the will *commits* a person, the proper movement of the heart *completely involves him at the deepest levels of*

his being. But still a challenge can be raised. What about the so called "Dark Night" we experience in the course of our spiritual and moral transformation, when we are void of all affectivity in our relationship with God? The answer to this question is that the "Dark Night" is itself *proof* that the affections give religious conversion its plenitude because the absence of affectivity is experienced precisely *as a trial.* When we are in the midst of such an experience we are aware that it ought not to be this way, although at the same time we can also see that there are certain fruits that can result from the successful endurance of such a trial, such as the strengthening of the will and an enlargement of the heart's ability to receive the proper affective gifts" (Father Adam Hertzfeld's summary of his *The Role of Spiritual Affectivity in Religious Conversion: A Study in the Life and Work of Dietrich von Hildebrand,* STD diss., Pontificia Universitas Lateranensis: Academia Alfonsiana, 2008).

31   See Blessed Columba Marmion, *Christ, The Life of the Soul* (St. Louis: Herder, 1925), 21-22.

32   Ponticus Evagrius, *Ad Monochus* (Manwah: Paulist Press, 2003).

33   Jeanne Heffernan, "Integrating Heart, Mind and Soul: The Vocation of a Christian Teacher," in John Dunaway, ed., *Gladly Learn, Gladly Teach* (Georgia: Mercer University Press, 2005), 116.

34   See Charles Murphy, *Models of Priestly Formation* (New York: Crossroad, 2006), 41ff; and *PPF* 22-25. Yves Congar highlighted the eschaton as being the theme that differentiates the monastic life from the diocesan priesthood. The eschaton, however, has arrived, and the pastor is realizing it in his ministering of the sacraments. It might be better to underscore the fact that the monk concentrates his service of God directly in the Church's liturgy, while the pastor mediates the mystery to everyday life in his commitment to becoming a contemplative even within his activity of pastoral charity.

35   Hans Urs Von Balthsar, *The Theology of Henri de Lubac* (San Francisco: Ignatius, 1991), 43.

36   "For a Christian, therefore, to pray is not to evade reality and the responsibilities it brings but rather, to fully assume them, trusting in the faithful and inexhaustible love of the Lord" (Pope Benedict XVI, Angelus, March 4, 2007).

Chapter Four

Teaching: Lecturing on Truth to Welcome Love

If any new models of contemplative seminary formation are to emerge, they will come from the seminary faculty and Bishop. One university professor, however, Catholic University of America theologian William Mattison appears to share this approach to contemplative teaching.

> Students seek not simply an intellectual grasp of relevant concepts or historical critical methods but a "hot" knowledge, which not only is grasped but also moves and influences.... [A]n encounter with the subject matter of theology should move them with conviction and not simply lead to greater understanding. Engaging students at the level of

faith means challenging them to intellectually explore questions whose answers are not achievable by one's intellect alone but require also an act of belief.[1]

Mattison continues:

What distinguishes an engaged from a disengaged theology class is the former's attention to the student's belief, rather than simply a recognition that religious phenomenon are worthy of serious study or that, out of respect for the faith identity of an institution, a certain corpus of texts or historical events warrants specific study. To not engage the students beyond this latter plane is not only a failure to present students with core life questions in a manner that indicates their significance; it is also an injustice to the material at hand.[2]

If this *university* professor can say all this, what *more* can seminary professors say? Further, Mattison recognizes some vital andragogical principles in teaching theology that assist the student in moving to a faith response. First, we need to be habituated by humility. Theologians approach the subject of their class knowing their minds cannot comprehend sufficiently the mystery of God and that faith must give to reason a fullness, a completion.[3] Faith gives the classroom theologian access to knowledge that changes the apprehension of truth. Without faith, one is simply a religious studies professor, not a theologian. Seminaries are established to be communities of theologians teaching in faith for the welfare of seminarian formation and the future welfare of Catholic parishioners.

Second, we need to relativize our own importance in the classroom.

> "God is the primary agent when engaging the faith of a student in the classroom. The teacher may 'feel' his words are not connecting but carries on because the Spirit is working; the teacher must pray and entrust his classes to God in prayer. The teacher is relativized but simultaneously dignified 'by taking part in that most beautiful encounter between a student and God.'"[4]

Deepening the students' union with God is primary, of course, but the eloquence of the theologian is also vital since we not only want our students to understand but to be moved. To teach a class in a beautiful way, a way that treasures rhetoric and language, is good andragogy. It is good because beauty synthesizes, or better, *is* a synthesis of all that is holy and good and true. We are moved by the beautiful because the synthesis has already happened or is happening within us.

Finally, we ought to teach with the hope that what we teach will facilitate our students' loving God more deeply. How do we teach with such hope? We teach out of our love of God and our love for our students for the sake of their love of God. Also, our life is a powerful element in calling forth a response from students; personal virtue, epistemology, and faith are intertwined. If Professor Mattison can be so bold in presenting these principles relative to teaching in a

Catholic university, might we be invited to even deeper freedom within our classes, a freedom that conspires with divine desire to move seminarians to deeper faith?

The integration of spirituality with academic theology is a *surrendered searching, a discerning abandonment,* or *a listening trust.* The terms *listening, discerning,* and *searching* imply a cognitive aspect in welcoming *truth,* whereas *surrender, abandonment,* and *trust* express the faith response of welcoming a *Person.* These two movements are not incongruent, but they have become somewhat separated today in the teaching of theology, when all there should be is a distinction. St. Paul understands spirituality to be the spirit-filled person possessing the obedience of faith (Romans 1:5)—a deep listening to Him who embodies the salvation mysteries. Here is the doorway into our teaching: We are to enter our vocation in faith and expect to come to know truth.

According to Paul Griffiths, "faith *is* a kind of reason." If this is true, then the core of spirituality *as surrender* is not to be somehow jury-rigged into academic theology but is *already present* as its heart. There are, of course, many other types of reasoning that have little or nothing to do with spirituality or surrender to the Paschal Mystery, such as the pragmatic skills that engineers and technicians need to master. Theology is not that kind of reasoning. Theology is born within a mind surrendered to the life, death, and resurrection of Christ. Theology is not the surrender itself, but it is born as a consequence of people abandoning themselves to Divine Mystery. Theology comes to life in the question, "Who have I surrendered to?" and the desire, "I want to know this God."[5] "Now this is eternal life, that they should know you, the only true God, and the one whom you sent, Jesus Christ" (John 17:3). Such desire for knowing God resides in the heart of the professor. This desire is not an addendum to teaching theology but its fuel, the source of our sustained commitment to teach the revelation of God. With each day that we labor for seminarians, we need to pray that desire is purified in us, protected in us, sustained in us by a familiarity with our own interiority. Alienation from interiority is bound to lead to theology becoming simply a subject we teach. Choosing to stay in the Presence, however, renders the texts we engage as places of renewal, healing, and inspiration.

Meditation

Can classroom teaching (lecture, discussion, and seminar) be a forum that intentionally aims students toward a knowledge that evokes a love of God? What would a faculty need to do to see that such an approach is more and more the norm?

Both seminarians and professors can become conscious of the stirrings of wonder within their hearts as classroom teaching is received or shared. Is there, however, a valid, *educational reason* to make these stirrings a communal reality or invite others to appropriate the content of a lecture at a deeper, more personal level of divine encounter? Griffiths notes:

> Because reason is for knowledge and knowl-
> edge is inherently relational, reason itself must
> be understood as inherently relational [oth-
> erwise knowledge is self-absorbed, ending in
> nihilism].... The pursuit of knowledge must
> be understood as a pursuit of communion....
> [G]enuine understanding is dialogical."[6]

Can the seminary classroom promote a dialogue
that includes an intentional reference to God's movement
in class, a movement known by those who are vulnerable to
truth, to those searching and discerning the truth? We know
that most parish priests do not read theology after ordination; they do read "spiritual" books, however. Why is that?
Could it be that they endured faculty lectures and books
simply because they were necessary for graduation? If we
have failed to instill a love for life-long learning in the field
in which they received their academic degrees, then why did
we labor so long at our desks and podiums? Maybe we mis-
understand the theological needs of priests? Maybe in buy-
ing popular spiritual books the parish priest is simply trying
to be *nourished by that which he desired all along, an affective
response to the God who personally called him to be engaged by
Truth.* Though we ought not to pander to the popular spirituality needs of seminarians in an academic setting, we must
serve the legitimate need of seminarians to know Christ in
study. Do we think this knowledge does not serve theology?
I am proposing that theologians suffer an encounter with
the Spirit *in* our study and *in* our teaching so that this Spirit
might particularize the doctrines we are teaching to the real
spiritual needs of seminarians.

To particularize the doctrine to the intellectual and spiritual hungers of the seminarian is uniquely the Spirit's work, and the Holy Spirit does not pander. Cooperating with this work of the Spirit requires us to give the Spirit space to enter; we need to invite the seminarian to welcome the Spirit when He prompts him during one of our lectures. To create such an environment of learning is far from pandering—it is an act of love for our students. We all know the caricature of the graduate studies professor who simply pushes content at the students, who dutifully write down whatever is said. When pressed to slow lectures down or review the material, the teacher laments, "There is so much for you to learn. I have no time to linger over the needs of individual persons, only time to share ideas." In fact, except for those with photographic memories, most of us cannot remember one lecture from our own graduate education. We might remember a professor, but remembering him or her only confirms my point: The *character* of the professor teaches implicitly in the classroom; his or her notes will always be available to consult and review. Some stellar lectures stand out in our minds, wisdom that we retain to this very day. Why is this?

Retaining such a memory indicates that the professor did not simply utter truth but uttered *truth for me*. The instructor taught in such a way that enabled me to receive the content and integrate it into my mind. Through the words of the professor, I was able to cooperate with the movements of the Holy Spirit within me. This approach is even more urgently needed in seminary, wherein the vocation being prepared for is dependent upon acquiring the same skill— the capacity to listen to the truth of a parishioner's life at levels that connect that life to the life of doctrine, the life of Christ's Mysteries, and to lead parishioners into those Mysteries. *Doctrine is living*, just like the seminarians we serve and the parishioners they will serve. Certainly some subjects will lend themselves more easily to contemplative methodologies than others, and prudence will dictate which need the emphasis I am giving and which will not. The same could be said of individual lectures that we prepare. We could go for weeks without a circumstance in our classroom routine that organically gives rise to silence, prayer, or meditation. I am not articulating an ideology, an agenda to which one is required to rigidly adhere, but an invitation to which one may freely respond, as the Spirit leads.

Some might think it is dangerous to develop a theological teaching method that is utilized mostly at seminaries, as distinct from university theology. After all, are we not all theologians? But not all theologians think that faith, prayer, and silence belong in the classroom. Many think that the only encounter in the classroom is limited to the class notes, notes as objects of study, and also fellowship with other students in the pursuit of truth. Beyond these contacts, however, many believe that contact with God in the classroom is to remain private. Since theology is fractured today, it would be disingenuous to pretend that some theologians are not really simply religious studies professors and have their reasons for remaining so.[7] Developing a more integrated method for teaching theology *in seminaries* is vital if we are to be faithful to God's call to raise up future priests who are prayerful theologians.

Meditation

As seminary professors, what fears operate in us that keep us from questioning our current teaching approach and setting forth in new directions (ancient directions, really)? Alternately, what values do seminary faculty protect in staying wedded to the theological content and method learned in their graduate education experience?

Teaching theology in a contemplative way orders seminarians to see the Word of God as a transformative event. This transformation is not normatively dramatic or immediate in its expression, but it should be expected. In other words, the spiritual conversion of our students is a conscious goal in seminary theology. Many university theologians do not want this; some do, but sadly, they feel the pressure from the majority of colleagues to discourage such diversity of teaching methods within the department. These professors suffer greatly, since they carry a more contemplative and personal approach to doing theology within their hearts.

Generally, however, such a contemplative approach to classroom teaching is characteristically different from university theology. University theology is ordered to different ends and serves many students whose Catholic faith is dormant. Most graduate schools are training future professors to replicate the present faculty. Therefore, in order to show the appropriate level of competence, graduate students are required to express what they know according to the method of the current professorial leadership. To define new ways of doing theology at the university level would take courageous leadership, leadership that acknowledges theology as a science explored within a transcendent relationship.

If seminarians are going to lead their parishioners into the spiritual life, then seminary theology must become free enough to welcome an encounter with God in the classroom. Seminary theology assists the seminarian in learning about God but also allows the formation staff to be visited by God in the form of *reverence before truth, silence that invites contemplation*, and *beauty revealed in doctrine and tradition*. To separate intimacy with God from the discipline of theology is to further advance the impotent trend of privatizing faith, relegating faith to the small places of the heart and leaving the public space of culture devoid of articulate and passionate priests. Public effects are born of what and who one loves. As noted previously, both the theologian and the seminarian stand to benefit from not *artificially preventing*, or from *conjuring* the presence of God that is manifested when two or more are gathered (Mt. 18:20). If the Catholic priesthood is to be healed of its contemporary wounds, it needs theologians to guide its candidates into healing encounters with the living Spirit and not simply introduce them to discursive and critical approaches to academic theology. The seminarian is being trained, after all, to one day be the dean of the school of prayer that is the parish.[8]

Virtue, as well as any approved faculty policies, will guide what types of responses are best for the promotion of prayer in the midst of public study. Certainly we have the right and duty to order such in our own classes, even to the point where no explicit prayer is encouraged. Obviously, we cannot stifle the Spirit from teaching silently within any particular student or even within our own hearts, meaning that note-taking in class can be an addendum to one's own spiritual journal.[9] What professor has not been instructed by the indwelling Spirit in the midst of lecturing, even to the point of sharing unplanned content? Most appealing, however, is when these inspired ideas lead to personal appropriation in the heart of the theologian. Teaching the truth changes not only our students but us as well.

Since prayer includes thinking we can prudently and rightfully speak of such thoughts in the classroom. Prayer can guide thought. Prayer is a form of love-imbued thinking ordered toward God, whom the theologian longs to know. Analogically, spouses think of their beloved often during the day and even at times share something of their love for their spouse with colleagues and friends. Love is public even if its *roots* and unutterable truths, appropriately remain private. Theology is not self-revelation but *contemplation of what God has revealed*, albeit *personally received* for the benefit of the Church. The seminarian can bear the fruit of this intimacy, and such fruit can be uttered, known, and shared to edify and serve the spiritual needs of parishioners. In seminary theology classrooms, seminarians can learn how to articulate their encounters with the divine.

As theologians, we are invited to approach the academic pillar of formation in a way that *draws out of the seminarian his love of God* and enables him to *contemplate such love when enacted in pastoral charity*. Can we teach in such a way that the desire for holiness in each seminarian is ignited from within the very intelligibility of theology?

> To be pastorally effective, intellectual forma-
> tion is to be integrated with a spirituality
> marked by a personal experience of God. In
> this way a purely abstract approach to knowl-
> edge is overcome in favor of that intelligence
> of heart which knows how "to look beyond,"
> and then is in a position to communicate the
> mystery of God to the people.[10]

For both Han Urs von Balthasar and St. Bonaventure, theology must be an affective science, moving the will and opening the person to transformation. "Let the experience of the
saint and not the average sinner be taken as the norm for
understanding the grace of the sacraments.... [T]heology
in the church proceeds always as continuous dialogue between bride and Bridegroom."[11] Theology *ultimately belongs
to those who are disposed toward the contemplative life, thus
creating a depth of meaning in the context of ministry, rooted
in one's abandonment to the Paschal Mystery in worship and
prayer.* Such a contemplative stance moves the seminarian
from intellect to heart to commitment. Theology is to perfect the knower of theology as a lover of God—that is what
Bonaventure means by it being an "affective" science.[12]

Meditation

*Are theologians "holy" enough to see the truth they want to share
with the seminarians? Are our seminarians fascinated enough
with the Holy so that they will continue their formation after
ordination?*

In the seminary, we can also say that *theology is a spirituality* as well as the source for developing one. Theology is a study of revelation that is *intentionally formational* and *structured to assist students in their call to "self-integration through self-transcendence."*[13] This integrative formation happens *in and through the mystery of Christ in the midst of His Church.* Since the spiritual life is the appropriation of revelation in practice, and since the spiritual life is always concrete and embedded within history, the spirituality of priestly theology is appropriately pursued through this question: In what way ought seminary professors *study, teach, and publish* theology in order to deepen the spiritual lives of priests and seminarians? Alternately, in what way ought seminarians and priests *receive the study, teachings, and publications* of seminary professors so as to deepen their appropriation of revelation in the service of their vocation?

To enter a contemplative theology is to enter a reasonable consideration of the event of all events: Reason has taken on flesh. Spirituality is not an abandonment of reason or the intellectual life, but reason is spirituality's object—the Christ, the *Logos.* As Justin Martyr said, "Reason became Man and was called Jesus Christ." We reason *from* Christ *to* other things, not *from* other things *to* Christ.[14]

One might argue persuasively that a theologian at a university should be concerned primarily with academic competence; however, that should never be said of a theologian in a seminary. Seminary professors must keep one eye on the scholarly task and one on formation's impact on the community of faith—this tension inheres in the future pastor. Seminary theology is about teaching and thinking from within an affirmation of faith, participating deeply within worship and prayer, and leading seminarians to pursue the "saintly intellect." This kind of intellect possesses affection for the person of Christ and is moved by Him as beloved object of Truth. The man who possesses the saintly intellect loves the Lord and wishes to introduce Him to the world by way of his pastoral charity and ministry. In this way seminary theology is founded upon conversion and an ever-deepening spiritual life that draws its life from worship, doctrine, and mission.

Pope Benedict XVI gives us valuable direction about seminary teaching in his address at the Gregorian University in 2006:

> [T]he immediate object of the different branches of theological knowledge is God himself, revealed in Jesus Christ, God with a human face. Even when, as in Canon Law and in Church History, the immediate object is the People of God in its visible, historical dimension, the deeper analysis of the topic urges us once again to contemplation, in the faith, of the mystery of the Risen Christ. It is he, present in his Church, who leads her among the events of the time towards eschatological fullness, a goal to which we have set out sustained by hope. However, knowing God is not enough. For a true encounter with him one must also love him. Knowledge must become love.
>
> The study of Theology, Canon Law and Church History is not only knowledge of the propositions of the faith in their

historical formulation and practical application, but is also always knowledge of them in faith, hope and charity. The Spirit alone searches the depths of God (cf. 1 Cor 2:10); thus, only in listening to the Spirit can one search the depths of the riches, wisdom and knowledge of God (cf. Rom 11:33). We listen to the Spirit in prayer, when the heart opens to contemplation of God's mystery which was revealed to us in Jesus Christ the Son, image of the invisible God (cf. Col 1:15), constituted Head of the Church and Lord of all things (cf. Eph 1:10; Col 1:18).[15]

This is an incredibly rich meditation by the pope for our present study. "Knowing God is not enough. For a true encounter with him one must also love him. Knowledge must become love." The pope even staves off any rejection of his argument by professors in the more practical theological disciplines when he reminds them to go deeper into the mystery of the Resurrection, as Christ is now filling the Church and its pastoral needs with His Spirit. "The Spirit alone searches the depths of God (cf. 1 Cor 2:10); thus, only in listening to the Spirit can one search the depths of the riches, wisdom and knowledge of God (cf. Rom. 11:33)."

Open-Mindedness

Many academics have counseled students to have an "open mind," not limited to the "traditional" ways of doing theology. I advocate a variant invitation: the times are calling us not to possess an open mind but a deeper mind. How then can we teach in ways that evoke a deeper mind, a heart open to the prayerful reception of truth? Perhaps we can look to the scriptural tradition of praying always (cf. Lk. 18:1; 1 Thes. 5:17) to assist our imagination in such a method of teaching. This deeper mind awaits those who welcome prayer within their heart as they work.[16] Gabriel Bunge's study of the desert fathers notes that the fathers "were not conducting a life of prayer alongside the rest of their life, but rather worked, like any other man, so as to make a living.... Their prayer life was identical with their daily life, permeating it completely ... so that [their] spirit is at prayer throughout the whole day."[17] As with our personal study, so it is and can be with our teaching; we welcome God by way of our sensitivity to the interior movements of the indwelling Spirit. If it can be said that we pray always, how does that influence our time in the classroom?

It would appear that prayer is impossible within the structure of class, a structure that is usually a rhythm of lecture on the theologian's part and listening on the part of the seminarian, with moments of conversation and questioning. I am advocating the inclusion of silent communion with the Spirit in the classroom as well, within which the truth can be more deeply appropriated. Is this spiritual give and take within the classroom a detriment to teaching? Theologians are not carpenters, able to fashion wood while simultaneously praying the Psalms or a series of Hail Marys. Our profession demands that the *mind be occupied* like the hands of a laborer. Where, then, is the "space" for prayer in teaching?

Clement of Alexandria (d. 215), early in the Christian tradition, noted how one might enter a life of praying always. "He prays, though, in all situations, whether he is taking a walk or with company or is resting or reading or beginning a task requiring thought. And he prays when in the very chamber of his soul he harbors just one thought and with sighs too deep for words invokes the Father, who is already present while he is still speaking."[18] The prayer that is unceasing is connected to the short, persistent prayers that desert monks uttered in times of temptation ("Lord, be merciful to me a sinner," etc.), but it is the interior prayer at the root of these utterings that is sustained, "always" running at a subconscious level, ever ready to be received as the Spirit "stirs the waters" of our soul (Jn. 5:7). In addition to personal prayer, our reflection upon and teaching of the truths of revelation carry great potential to stir the waters of the soul. Within our very teaching, at the moment of our speaking, we can be invited to enter prayer. Prayer within our lecture is not only "short persistent utterances" but descriptions of mystery, questions to further understanding, and silence to promote attentive responses to the seminarians' inquiries or summations.

Normally, according to academic habit, we resist such invitations to prayer as being imprudent. As noted above, not all interior movements of prayer should become public in the classroom. We can silently give praise to God for the graces being received in the midst of lecturing without any student ever knowing. Now, however, we arrive at the white-hot center of our discussion. Is there a time during a public lecture when the professor, having already personally accepted the invitation to pray, invites the seminarians into prayer as well? What would this prayerful reception of doctrine mean academically? How would we protect individual freedom within the class? Alternately, how would we delight in the fact that such prayer can guide the intellect?[19]

> [I]f reason is to be exercised properly, it must undergo constant purification, since it can never be completely free of the danger of a certain ethical blindness caused by the dazzling effect of power and special interests....
>
> Faith by its specific nature is an encounter with the living God—an encounter opening up new horizons extending beyond the sphere of reason. But it is also a purifying force for reason itself. From God's standpoint, faith liberates reason from its blind spots and therefore helps it to be ever more fully itself. Faith enables reason to do its work more effectively and to see its proper object more clearly.[20]

Here we see the great truth: Faith, received as prayer, helps us to think clearly. Let us invite faithful prayer to be a source of objective theological thinking and banish from our minds the notion that it should remain operative only on the level of private study.

> Since the object of theology is the Truth which is the living God and His plan for salvation revealed in Jesus Christ, the theologian is called to deepen his own life of faith and continuously unite his scientific research with prayer. In this way, he will become more

open to the "supernatural sense of faith" upon which he depends, and it will appear to him as a sure rule for guiding his reflections and helping him assess the correctness of his conclusions.

Through the course of centuries, theology has progressively developed into a true and proper science. The theologian must therefore be attentive to the epistemological requirements of his discipline, to the demands of rigorous critical standards, and thus to a rational verification of each stage of his research. The obligation to be critical, however, should not be identified with the critical spirit which is born of feeling or prejudice. The theologian must discern in himself the origin of and motivation for his critical attitude and allow his gaze to be purified by faith. The commitment to theology requires a spiritual effort to grow in virtue and holiness.[21]

In a contemplative theology that is at home in the seminary, we will find the presence of God emerging from the material taught and from within the communion known between teacher and seminarian. In this approach to teaching, we are not only or always arguing a case, but instead we are welcoming a Presence, "quite different from scientific argument but not anti-intellectual."[22] In a contemplative theology we become vulnerable to receive what emerges. This receptivity is not purely passive but the fruit of a surrendered searching. In such surrender the professor is not looking to "tackle" concepts like prey, but to actively wait as a hunter in a blind for the prey to emerge. Professors watch and wait in hope that truth will emerge and be interiorized by their students. The professor wants truth to emerge in class and expose its elemental structure, a structure that invites seminarians to participate in its reality unto communion with and rest in meaning.

In our era, the scientific method brackets out the mysterious and religious. We in the seminary embrace mystery so as to better serve our end: the formation of mystical-pastoral priests. The seminarian suffers the Presence that emerges from within his meditation upon the content of class. In this way we call him not simply to "work" at study to achieve academic "success," but to watch and wait and receive the Presence *in study*, finding a rest that gives birth to wisdom.

This kind of learning has echoes in the mystic education of Edith Stein, Jacques Maritain, and John Henry Newman. Michael Buckley notes that these thinkers did not enter a new depth of thinking by simply following the historical-critical method or other "scientific" approaches but by receiving the call to holiness from within a study of the saints. It is the saints who point to the culmination of all ratiocination—communion with the divine. Buckley states:

> If what these histories [lives of the saints] point to is true, is it not extraordinary that so much Christian formal theology for centuries has bracketed this actual witness as of no intellectual weight.... Is it not a lacuna in the standard theology, even of our day, that theology neither has nor has striven to forge the intellectual devices to probe in these concrete

experiences the disclosure they offer of the
reality of God and so render them available
for so universal a discipline?[23]

Buckley explains that one of the few exceptions to this is the
work of Saint John of the Cross, who expressed religious experience *in* his writings. Can we express religious experience,
not bracket it out, in our theological teaching? If the art of
poetry in the writings of Saint John of the Cross can carry
theological truth as encounter, I am sure the art of teaching
can carry it as well.

Classroom Lecture

How might we approach teaching so that religious
experience is disclosed and not hidden? In integrating spirituality with our theological teaching, we need to consider:

1. The faith of the professor, which must be made
    active in teaching.

2. The faith of the seminarian, which must be made
    active in learning.

3. The content of theology, which may be inten-
    tionally ordered toward a response in prayer.

4. The content of theology, which may also be or-
    dered toward a response in pastoral charity. Here
    we acknowledge that ministry is the fruit of
    priestly study and prayer.

We should also consider how we approach explicit class-room prayer.

1. The opening prayer of each class, beyond the perfunctory, can be ordered toward a contemplative reception of theology by the students. Prayer can awaken the seminarian to receive the content of class as seeds for growth in pastoral charity, and also as a privileged location for intimacy with Christ.

2. The closing prayer of the class is an act of faith which gathers together the fragments of the lecture and conversation ordering the students to contemplate what has been received. Such a prayer reinforces the content of the class and drives it into the heart, the memory. In this way the content and graces of class can be visited later in memory.

3. The object of seminary academic formation ought to be conducive to forming priests responsive to the holy, fascinated with it, enabling them to lead others into a similar stance as well. Seminary theology also serves this object as its end.

4. At the end of each class, or minimally at the end of each semester of teaching, the professor ought to ask the seminarian to identify which theme within the lectures or texts ignited or sustained a spiritual conversion within him.

The vital prerequisite for allowing the Presence to emerge in our teaching is found in our own vulnerability to truth as it personally approaches and claims our hearts. Buckley quotes Simon Weil, who notes that truth is her guide, and that even if one were to turn away from Christ in faith and go only "toward truth, one will not go far before falling into His arms."[24]

Pastoral Effects

Personal communication with God in the midst of study will help us foster a generation of priests able to identify and welcome God in events that appear to be "only secular" in nature. Most importantly, it will aid in keeping future priests reading and studying theology long after ordination, because they will know that God meets them in such learning. Karl Adam, the German theologian who died in 1996, was certainly known as a giant intellect. His books are erudite, and when first written, they were considered prophetic in many ways. What is less known is that when he taught the fullness of what he saw in his intellect, it moved his heart to such a point that it became evident to his students. Bernard Häring, the twentieth-century moral theologian, reported the following after attending one of Adam's lectures: "Not seldom we, his students, could see tears in his eyes when he spoke on the true humanity of Christ, the Living Word of God."[25] How beautiful to be so open to truth that it moves a professor's entire being and becomes an icon of the mission of theology for his students.

This capacity for truth to move us is crucial to reflect upon and welcome within a seminary setting, since the end of all seminary formation is to prepare a man to be moved by pastoral desire and become committed to its proper end: serving the needs of the poor. This desire, however, is only firmly established upon a personal vulnerability to Christ, the Truth, as Karl Adam displayed. If we are to lecture so as to welcome love within our own heart and the hearts of our students, then such lecturing must be expectant in its discernment of Truth. To teach with such expectation is to teach in hope, trusting in the promise that God has come and is coming in Christ to heal His people. Such a coming cannot be calculated but is only a grace. Desiring such a coming, however, is the ground to receive the same.

Making room in the classroom to know God through *the discipline* of seminary study assists the student and professor to be disposed to receive a divine encounter in the same way that the death of selfishness prepares them for a personal encounter with another. (Of course, these two movements can be one.) Study and the commitment to it as a way of life can heal the ego not only because of the ascetic commitment involved but also because the Object of theological study facilitates healing. If the seminarian remains vulnerable to God's truth and seeks its effect upon his will, then spiritual, moral, and intellectual healing (as opposed to receiving a physical cure from an ailment) will occur. In this way the seminarian is training to be the physician of the soul. Such training is the result of the seminarian *knowing* a life of interiority by what he suffers in his own conversion and by what he suffers in study as he encounters the power of divine revelation.

Meditation

"Here we see the great truth: Faith, received as prayer, helps us to think clearly." Could we invite prayer and faith to be sources of objective theological thinking and banish from our current thinking the notion that they should remain operative only on the level of private study?

Such desire for truth will anchor the seminarian within any method of seminary theology. Such desire will free theology, in other words, to receive its ultimate end: a prayerful union of mind and will, giving birth to ministry. He studies theology to mediate its healing truth, not to become an "academic," still less to gain personal prestige or power. Seminary curriculum ought to render the seminarian and professor more vulnerable to the call of personal conversion, not less. Any teaching system or methodology employed ought to be reviewed with this end in mind: Has such a method yielded deep, personal conversions from error and sin? Further, has such study oriented the teacher and student toward communion with Christ and ministry within His Church?

In a seminary, such formation goals can be accomplished by both the professor and seminarian when they enter the discipline of study to become *weak before the promptings* of the Holy Spirit. This way of learning combines the asceticism of precise research with the affection for yielding to the promptings of the Spirit. With such yielding, a wisdom *born of study* but *not identical to its content* emerges. In this kind of approach we are open to cultivating that deeper mind, a mind that treasures contemplative ways of receiving truth, truths that heal the Church because they flow from communion with the Mystery of Divine Love.[26]

Notes

1 William Mattison, ed., *New Wine, New Wineskins: A Next Generation Reflects on Key Issues in Catholic Moral Theology* (Lanham: Sheed & Ward, 2005), 80.

2 Ibid., 82.

3 Ibid., 88.

4 Ibid., 89.

5 Paul J. Griffiths and Reinhard Hutter, ed., *Reason and the Reasons of Faith: Theology for the Twenty-First Century* (New York: T&T Clark, 2005), 11ff.

6 Griffiths and Hutter, *Reason and the Reasons of Faith*, 19.

7 Obviously, we may be seeing a growing hospitality to faith in the classroom in the likes of Professor Mattison and his generation of theologians.

8 John Paul II, "The Eucharist as a School of Prayer," *Origins* 28, (April 8, 1999): 729.

9 See Appendix for one model we can use to encourage our students to receive the content of class in a more contemplative manner.

10 Pope John Paul II, *PDV* 51, 1992.

11 Gregory La Nave, *Through Holiness to Wisdom: The Nature of Theology according to St. Bonaventure* (Rome: Istituto storico dei cappuccini, 2005), 215.

12 La Nave, *Through Holiness to Wisdom*, 222.

13 Sandra Schneiders, "A Hermeneutical Approach to the Study of Christian Spirituality," in Elizabeth Dreyer, ed., *Minding the Spirit* (Baltimore: Johns Hopkins University Press, 2004), 51.

14 See Robert Louis Wilken, *The Spirit of Early Christian Thought* (New Haven: Yale University Press, 2005), 15.

15 "Visit of the Holy Father to the Pontifical Gregorian University," *Address Of His Holiness Benedict XVI*, Friday, November 3, 2006. *http://www. vatican.va/holy_father/benedict_xvi/speeches/2006/november/documents/ hf_ben-xvi_spe_20061103_gregoriana_en.html*

16 Gabriel Bunge, *Earthen Vessels* (San Franciso: Ignatius, 2002), 105-123. See also Bernard Lonergan, *Collected Works of Bernard Lonergan*, ed. Robert Croken, et al. (Toronto: University of Toronto Press, 2004), 179: "But this life of grace within us can become a habitual conscious living. When I say 'habitual' I mean that one is not thinking of it all the time but that one easily reverts to it, that one can be, as it were, distracted from worldliness in as easy and as spontaneous a manner as when one in love is distracted from everything except the beloved. It is not a matter of study of oneself or analysis

of oneself. It is a living, a developing, a growing, in which one element is gradually added to another and a new whole emerges. That transformation is the mediation of what is immediate in us. What is immediate in us is that *de facto* we are temples of the Holy Spirit, members of Christ, and adoptive children of the Father, but in a vegetative sort of way. That can move into our conscious living, into our spontaneous living, into our deliberative living; and that is growth in prayer."

17 Bunge, *Earthen Vessels*, 110.

18 As quoted in Bunge, *Earthen Vessels*, 112.

19 Congregation for the Doctrine of the Faith, *Instruction on the Ecclesial Vocation of the Theologian* 8, 1990.

20 Pope Benedict XVI, *Deus Caritas Est* 28.

21 CDF, *Ecclesial Vocation of the Theologian* 8, 9.

22 Michael J. Buckley, SJ, *Denying and Disclosing God: The Ambiguous Progress of Modern Atheism* (New Haven: Yale University Press, 2004), 125.

23 Ibid., 130.

24 Ibid., 132.

25 See Robert Kreig, *Karl Adam* (South Bend: University of Notre Dame Press, 1992), 155.

26 The love of God can certainly determine what we do pastorally and shape our judgments. "[W]hen we have ordinate affections from the love of charity, our love of God shapes our practical judgments.... In the gift of wisdom ... the intellect becomes receptive to the action of the Holy Spirit.... The intellect specifies our acts, but it is moved to engage in this specifying by the charity present in the will." It is incumbent upon theologians to insure that seminarians *think out of what they love and love what is worthy to be held in contemplation*. See Michael Sherwin, *By Knowledge and By Love* (Washington, DC: Catholic University of America Press, 2005), 235-237.

Chapter Five

Worship: Adoring the Mystery that Fascinates Us

One can conclude, then, that for Ephraem, when one reads the Bible, one does not engage in theology "in the Augustinian sense of fides quarens intellectum," but in a theology of contemplation, "fides adorans mysterium." The point of reading the Bible for Ephraem is to "induce silence in response to awesome wonder."

Mary Sheridan
"St. Ephraem: 'Faith Adoring the Mystery'"

I f we are open to the promptings of the Holy Spirit in our teaching and study, then we have already entered worship. The seminary professor who loves to study the Word because of who he or she will

149

find there is a teacher who longs to impart a way of living, a pattern of life that feeds the soul. This theologian has become "pastoral" in the fullest sense of the word. We know what pastures feed our sheep because, led by the Spirit, we have grazed there ourselves. We are in fact driven to these pastures, pastures that might console or, as they were for Christ, pastures that are a desert (cf. Mt. 4:1-11; Lk. 4:1-13), void of consolation but necessary in *some way* to hone our mind or will in the journey to holiness. As contemplative theologians, our worship is never separate from study,[1] and study is always the place to have our love-imbued mind fed with the truth of God, whether that study is a burden or a delight, a desert of discipline or a field of plenty. Beyond the presence of prayer in our study and teaching, how does explicit worship intersect with our vocation of seminary professor?

Jean Corbon invites us into a beautiful and deeply moving exposition of worship in his work, *The Wellspring of Worship*. His writing helps us to see how our seminary work relates to our participation in the worship of the Church. Corbon meditates upon the flowing source of life and love, which is the Father and the Father's gift of His Son, Jesus, communicated through the Holy Spirit by virtue of Mary's "Yes." We are called to enter this flowing river of love and allow it to carry us back to the source, the Father's love for all human beings. We worship Christ because, as God, He willed to enter death for us; in so doing He shattered its hold over the human race, a hold that encompasses our physical, spiritual, moral, and affective lives. Christ wholly entered death and thus, as the God-Man, invites us wholly into His

way, His self-donation upon the cross, a cross that offers freedom from sin and death by virtue of the light of the resurrection. This great mystery beguiles and fully fascinates the
seminary theologian. The theologian is offered salvation, as
are all persons, but this offer is received within a *specific vocation to contemplate revelation and salvation* in the context of
forming future priests.

As theologians, we are like the Samaritan woman
whom Jesus invites to a deeper level of knowledge (Jn. 4:4ff).
Resting in this knowledge, we find our mission by meditating upon the truths of revelation. We are thus invited, by
way of an interior desire, to rest only in a life of contemplation and of continuing that contemplation in the presence
of our students. In our vocation we meditate upon both the
Source of life-giving waters (revelation) and the effects such
a gift has upon those who drink in such a Spirit (pastoral
desire). Paradoxically, this *work* of meditation is a *true rest*, a
true vocation for the theologian.[2] In our intellectual and affective communion with the mystery of Christ, we find our
purpose. We yield to this call (perhaps only after restlessly
searching elsewhere), and our lives become an intellectual
offering to and promotion of the mission of the Church.

When we worship, we are taken up into our vocation's true end and object: participation in the Paschal Mystery. We do not critique, question, or explore theological
data while participating in the Eucharistic liturgy; rather,
theology itself enters us. We receive the Mystery of Christ
within our vulnerable heart—open to receive and eager to
be affected by so great a divine love. The effects of such vul-

nerability deepen our desire to know the gift, to know the one who is giving and is given (Jn. 4:10).

Our call is not only to enter the death of Christ as *the source* of our salvation, but also quite uniquely to enter it as the source of our mission of teaching and reflection. Worship is the place where theologians are born—where our hearts, our interiority, are awakened, nourished and guided. Successfully navigating the complex matrix of the academy is not the primary guide for the theologian; only drinking deeply from the well of Christ's living water can orient us. As a result of learning a contemplative theology born of and open to worship, the seminarian will be compelled, out of love, to invite his future parishioners to pay attention to the mystery of salvation.

A priest who so bids his people is not an authoritarian cleric but a truly invitatory presence. A priest formed by contemplative theology guides his people to look within—to listen, to pray, to attend to the Mystery that seeks to define their entire lives. Seminarians who study in the presence of theologians who define themselves by worship look for rest only in the holy, not simply in the expedient or practical. This fruit is then shared with future parishioners and presented to them with longing: If you only knew the gift that God is sharing with you (cf. Jn. 4:10). This fascination with holiness is not to be understood as elitist but a holiness born of our journey to humility. It is a journey mapped out by theologians who teach the kenotic mystery of Christ, one that bids the priest and theologian to enter the holy by way of the *mandatum*, serving at table (cf. Jn. 13:15). What we behold in worship, and what fires our imagination, inexorably leads to availability, not seclusion or elitism. Only the perverse, the pathological, are led from worship to seclusion, elitism, or ideology. Rather, the one who *suffers the entrance of mystery* is always led to a life of contemplation and service.

We, then, are bid to pay attention to the Source of Christ's own gift, the Eucharistic liturgy. We are to worship there to receive grace, the life of God that comes to inhabit the soul. It is our dignity to host the presence of Christ's own self-offering upon the cross within our hearts.

From such interiority a healing flows within the theologian, a spiritual healing that affects any needed emotional healing. As professors of the Word, we do not want our unhealed ideologies, prejudices, or familial wounds to be unconsciously inflicted upon the seminarian. As formators in the seminary, it is our duty to be open to the depths of our soul in all honesty and humility, and to receive the healing that Christ wants to give. "Of course I will it" (cf. Mk. 1:41). Only the healed person is truly *free* to explore and be explored by Revelation. In being so available, we welcome Christ in worship and allow Him to grip our heart in fascination, a fascination that will be shared in teaching and writing. In worship we pay direct attention to the mystery, while at our desk we welcome the grace of worship to secure any further encounters with the always-flowing mystery of salvation. St. Therese of Lisieux noted:

> I have never heard [God] speak, yet I know
> he is within me. He is there, always guiding
> and inspiring me; and just when I need them
> most, lights hitherto unseen, break in upon

me. This is not as a rule during my prayers,
but in the midst of my daily duties.[3]

Here St. Therese so clearly acknowledges that prayer alights
upon us, alights upon those who aspire to a state of openness, a life of communion with God. The Fathers of the
Second Vatican Council noted that one of the greatest errors of our time is the separation of faith from everyday life.[4]
St. Therese would find such a separation foreign. Seminary
theologians ought to work and live in opposition to that error and contribute to its mending by emptying themselves
to receive the graces of worship whenever and wherever they
appear in prayer.

Meditation

*The greatest error of academic theology today is the separation of
prayer and worship from its content and expression. What kind
of theology emerges from worship and how is it sustained and
furthered in the classroom?*

Attendance at the Eucharistic liturgy is essential for
the seminary theologian. Those in love *want* to accompany
each other; they do not compel the other to pay attention.
Communion with Christ is established and deepened by
frequent participation in the Eucharistic liturgy. The effects
of such worship are real enough to heal us even if we do not

attend formal worship every day. Beyond worship, however, we should ask to be healed: "As I attend now to Your Word in study, may such an encounter promote the healing of my disordered loves."

If we teach seminarians out of our love for the Eucharistic mystery, then theology can heal, and our lecture notes, books, and articles can be "leaves of healing" as well (Rev. 22:2). Here, in our *product*, our lectures and writings, our own "thirst for truth"[5] co-mingles with God's thirst for communion with the Church in worship. From within our participation in the Paschal Mystery, we surrender to the desire of God to take our writings and lectures and to define them. As a result of this yielding, we can teach with power, in faith, out of our intimacy with Christ. In other words, the classroom lecture becomes and remains the *fruit* of prayerful gratitude, even as it remains porous to prayer *presently emerging* within class or at the research desk. "Christ, if I have never thanked You before, I thank You now, for inviting me into the mission of forming priests." By being open to prayer alighting upon the consciousness during study and teaching, and by receiving God from within the affections, theologians give witness to this same divine companionship within the seminarian's future ministry as well. In connecting the study of theology with worship, we give such study our full attention—we give ourselves over to the truth of its content and host its power to convert. This is theology undertaken in its fullness.

By integrating theological study, teaching, and a personal call to worship, we allow the heart of Christ to enter us. The heart of Christ enters the heart of the theologian over and over, each time consent is given. The place of the passion of God, Christ's own heart now enters the theologian's heart.[6] Attending to God in Christ, we contemplate the very fountain of our mission. We want the heart of God—Christ—to become our own (Gal. 2:20). Christ is God's desire for Man and Man's desire for God *satisfied*. As seminary theologians, we offer our own love-imbued hearts as a place for this mystery to inhabit. We give the saving mystery of Christ our full attention and so fulfill our vocation.

In making this offer, the theologian acknowledges that Western culture is "dying of prayer-lessness," that it is existing in an age of distraction, an age of confusing the means of life with the end or purpose of life. The theologian recognizes that persons are pulled apart in their affections, many unable to alight anywhere, fearful that they will miss the next new thing or experience. It is a culture devoid of Sabbath, where few find relationships within which to rest. Out of a converted interiority, out of the suffering we undergo to become theologians, we can gift seminarians with a reverence for communion with the Holy and move them away from an existence of distraction. As contemplative theologians, we share with the seminarians how the mystery of Christ in the Eucharist came to heal our own distracted lives, and we summon them to gaze upon the beauty of God's gift of self in Christ. The seminarians are invited to the peace received in moving from a life of distraction to one full of the promise born of paying attention to Christ.[7] In other words, they are invited to enter a formation that moves them into prayer (attention) and away from anxiously awaiting the next new trend (distraction).

The more God gives Himself, the more He reveals Himself. Thus, we must be involved in the place where God is given if we are to receive the revelation that occupies the work of the profession. The Eastern church expresses the theological task as emerging from a mind concentrated in the heart. Our heart is to be formed and affected by the revelation in which we participate at worship. In worship, the scholar is taken up into the self-offering of Christ upon the Cross and the life-giving response of the Father in the resurrection. In this giving by Christ, we receive our salvation and linger in intellectual and affective fascination over the graciousness of such a gift. We must be taken up in the divine self-offering if we are to understand the revelation. Theology without worship is anemic. There is no blood in it, no life.

Out of the power of worship, the theologian's mind is ordered toward encounter and communion. The mind of such a theologian serves the student by always teaching within and toward the mystery of the Eucharistic liturgy. The liturgy is the place of encounter, the place of communion with Christ today. The work of the Holy Spirit that we welcome at Mass operates primarily by purifying our hearts from within so that we might *receive* Christ. Worship allows us to be known by Christ. Each time we worship, the heart softens to allow the Spirit to affect our decision-making more and more. Theologians then seek to discern in the Spirit. Not allowing the mind or affections to be overly distracted about the minutiae of scholarly method, we are eager to point students to where the Paschal Mystery is breaking into our studies. We want the work of the Holy Spirit—an inexhaustible pedagogy—to be conducted within us, so that in turn we can tutor the seminarian in the new ways of the Lord. In the actual teaching of theology, the Spirit searches the mind of the students and teacher so as to illuminate the content of class to reveal where "the Lord is coming ... at the heart of every event."[8]

If theology class is to be embraced as an extension of the Liturgy of the Word, then its call for silence after the homily must be heeded in the classroom as well. As noted above, the classroom lecture becomes and remains the *fruit* of prayerful gratitude. Within such gratitude exists a desire to remain porous to prayer, to welcome God as He *presently emerges* within class or at the research desk. Prayer emerges, as does all communication, most profoundly out of silence.

Romano Guardini meditated upon the rhythm of silence and speaking that exists at the heart of God, a giving and receiving in the Spirit between the Father and Son.[9] God occasionally uses silence to indicate His presence (1 Kg. 19:11ff). The silence that envelops us in God's presence is different from what Guardini calls "natural interiority." The divine silence is one filled with life, a kind of silence we need to learn to receive. Due to our pragmatism and our utilitarian sense of education, we often fight against this depth of encounter and resist entering the Presence it conveys. And yet, when truth is uttered and received in a theology class, it oftentimes takes a student's breath away and bears him into deeper participation by way of a graced silence. Here the truth is silencing the mind by the sheer force of its compelling beauty. We can choose to receive this silently wrapped beauty, or we can rush on, seeking to escape its conversion power with more lecturing. All words that seek to hasten us away from this enveloping silence might rightly be called "chatter," because our class had come to the point of encounter and we chose to escape it. Students and professors ought to *expect* this visitation of truth wrapped in the silence of divine encounter. This is normal for theology but abnormal for academia; therefore, silence must be learned.

Meditation

While studying, we all pause and grow silent when truth enters our heart. We may even allow this truth to take us to the Person of Christ. How would following this pattern in the classroom facilitate learning?

Guardini points to the freedom found in silence: "We must be serious about this. A life properly lived includes the practice of silence.... We must learn that silence is beautiful, that it is not emptiness, but true and full of life.... In doing this we shall make a great discovery: that the interior world of man is spacious and admits of ever deeper penetration."[10] In silence the dawn of truth is breaking. By inviting the silence, the students and professors recognize that Someone has emerged in the class, that there is a Presence gently bearing the means of communion. This Presence stirs the student and moves his affections in the face of the intellect's grasp of truth. The still, small sound has rustled the Spirit into our consciousness, and now He seeks to enlighten us by the truth and seeks communion with those who welcome it in silent reception.

Such a reception does not have to be overtly dramatic or unduly extended, but it will only affect the conversion of the participants if given time to enter the soul and adhere to the will by a stirring of affection. In theology class such a silence can be collectively entered in the same way a congregation would receive it after a moving homily. The liturgical rubrics give the community time to rest in silence after the homily. The presider may fail to surrender to these opportunities, however, which is a loss to the community in its quest to deepen a mystic consciousness. Even though there are no written rubrics for theology class perhaps we can allow virtue to call us to yield to a *silent appropriation of truth*. The seminary, above all, should heed this call because it is, by its very nature, a community of men defined by and identified with worship.

"Speak, for your servant is listening" (1 Samuel 3:10) ought to be the emblem of seminary theology, as it sums up the stance of both seminarian and professor—a stance of humility before truth and a confidence that silent prayer does not threaten academic study. Thus, we want to encourage the seminarian to discern the truth as it issues forth from silence. Growing familiarity with silence is crucial to the seminarian's development of pastoral acumen—around times of grief with parishioners, around times of hospitality with strangers, around times of fullness in prayer at the liturgy and personal prayer alone or with others. The priest ought to be an expert in leading others into a full, living silence, because he has been formed in its riches at the seminary.

When I suggest that spiritual realities such a prayer, silence, and contemplation be integrated into academic venues, a common fear can arise that these elements may make the academy a place of "uncontrolled" emotion, that an ecstatic prayer meeting may replace education. One element of Catholic worship assists in calming such fears: the Eucharistic liturgy itself is sober. Corbon notes this: "As for the sacramental 'signs,' their sobriety is the best condition for letting the mystery shine through and for making it visible to our receptive faith."[11] Calling for a new kind of classroom filled with the activity of a prayer meeting, for example, would misconstrue the intention of my proposal. Rather, to let worship influence and exist in the teaching and study of theology is to let the *character* of Catholic worship define such learning methods.

The guiding principle in the classroom, then, is pedagogical sobriety. This disposition matches the dignity of our worship, which allows Christ to emerge out of sacramental signs. In the case of the classroom, the signs are the beauty and truth of the doctrine, spoken in words. The seminarians are not onlookers or spectators at an entertaining lecture but active, conscious participants in the truth unfolding in the classroom. As noted before, the Holy Spirit conspires with the class members and professor to bring them all to a disposition of humility before truth. By way of the sober methods of the classroom, this conspiracy can have the effect of Encounter—not sacramental but, nonetheless, intellectually, affectively, and spiritually transformational. What the theology classroom bears is not *salvation* by way of signs but *conversion* by way of signs: words and fellowship that potentially carry an encounter with Truth. In such a forum, enthusiasm does not rule the environment, only the rest known in surrendering to the affectively-imbued intellect as it welcomes truth.

Meditation

Beyond the communal participation of the seminary community at daily liturgies, what practices might sustain the personal connection between worship and learning? Is there anything intentional that can be done to deepen the mysteries of Christ within theologians, not simply as believers but as believers who carry the mission of theologian?

Praying Together

There was a theory voiced once that *the way* the Quakers prayed—a silent group listening for truth—led them to reject slavery as a moral option long before many other religious groups.[12] Prayer carries with it the potential to hear truth, a truth emerging from the soul. If theologians prayed in an *intentional manner*, would the truth enter them at deeper and regular rates of breathing, becoming a part of their deepest desires? There is, of course, the daily praying of the Liturgy of the Hours, but the approach to prayer that I am recommending here is more specifically vocational, more focused upon the graces we need to search the Word *as intellectuals* and bear the fruits of that search in the classroom. My approach to seminary theology invites professors to let spirituality lead their study and teaching. This approach complements Augustine's "faith seeking understanding" but is truly an explication of St. Emphraem's "faith adoring the mystery" of Christ. If we approach theology in faith and adoration, regular informal prayer among the theology faculty will assist in keeping this consciousness alive; our mission would stand uniquely as the intention of our prayer.

Outside of formal liturgical prayer where the heart aligns with the needs of the whole Church, any prayer that is mission-centered or informally drawn up by the faculty calls for mutual trust. Trust of one another, or at least the desire to have trust restored or discovered, is the prerequisite desire if a more intentional and personal prayer life among the faculty is to be constituted. The specific type of prayer I am advocating encourages all to enter such prayer in trust. This prayer places an emphasis upon the *mission of the theologian* before God; it is not a general prayer meeting.

If the faculty is divided ideologically along political lines, such prayer may assist in the healing of the faculty as they focus upon what unites them: a faith in Christ that leads to adoration, a kneeling of the intellect before divine Truth. If there are divisions within the faculty over doctrinal or moral teachings, or intra-ecclesial politics, so to speak, these may be more stubborn to heal. In this case, perhaps time spent in prayer and fasting under the leadership of the dean or rector might be appropriate. After such time and by way of the rector's discernment, a regular schedule of mission prayer may be established. Without such a condition, the personal distrust between faculty members will inhibit their availability to each other and to God in one another's presence.

In the beginning such prayer might happen once or twice a month. Greater frequency is needed at the beginning of new spiritual exercises, or they will never take root habitually. These gatherings would be presided over by a single faculty member in charge of creating or acquiring the content of the prayer. Such a prayer would work best at a convenient time in the daily schedule and last no longer than twenty minutes. As these prayer gatherings become established in the habits of participating faculty members, time may be adjusted.

It would be best if the method of prayer centered upon a version of *lectio divina*, thus supporting the method of research and teaching I am advocating. The faculty could pray with a relevant text about the mission of the theologian or the nature of theology (e.g. Jn. 16:13; 1 Tim. 6:16; 1 Pt. 3:15; Jn. 8:32; Lk. 10:21f). Perhaps a germane portion of the Liturgy of the Hours could be used, such as the Office of Readings. After the text is read three times, interspersed with moments of silence, a greater silence is entered into by the faculty. Here we simply want to receive the mystery of our mission, the dignity of our work, and some aspect of the reality of Christ's identity or His Church. After the silence, the presider will intone spontaneous or prepared prayers of the faithful or some appropriate response to the reading along the lines of the Responsorial Psalm in the Liturgy of the Word. Then each faculty member, if desired, can respond to the reading or add a prayer of intercession. St. Philip Neri used to listen to the Word of God and attend to the specific text where his heart came to rest. He would then meditate upon that word in a way disposed to prayer. Such a style of meditation is appropriate in this forum of theologians as well.

This common prayer is an effort to allow Christ to personally move the participants. I do not envision it in any way replacing the Liturgy of the Hours, wherein the *objective* Word is received and treasured. As academics, however, it is very easy for theologians to be overly discursive or analytical even in their prayer. Presiders may want to invite their peers to receive the mission of theology and Christ's presence at a personal level. This can be done by inviting all present to speak to Christ personally, allowing the silences to envelop each participant. Out of the silence emerges a personal cry to Christ, one filled with adoration, thanksgiving, intercession, or other movements that lead the professor to know who Christ is and what He brings specifically to theologians. Obviously if we do not enter into a prayer of the heart it will be considerably more difficult for us to moderate the silences and prayers that emerge from our own study and classroom teaching. This forum of faculty prayer is meant to reinforce the unity of theology, faith, and prayer. We are called to ask God for the grace to avoid separating what He has joined: the love-imbued intellect receiving truth in faith.

Since each of us prays on our own or within the liturgies of the Church, such a discretional gathering does not constitute the essential component of contemplative theology. It may, however, enhance faculty fellowship, common mission, and spiritual insight, since Christ promised to be with those who pray in His name. John Henry Newman struggled with his own personal prayer, but he knew the value of such a struggle, as it indicated the displacement of a mind lodged in this passing age and the emergence of a mind that attends to Christ. He notes this: "My God ... my heart goes after shadows. I love anything better than communion with Thee. I am ever eager to get away from Thee. Often I find it difficult to even say my prayers.... Teach me to love prayer. Teach me to love that which must engage my mind for all eternity."[13]

Study and teaching may open up to include prayer, even eventually become prayer, but in themselves they are not prayer. Prayer must still be attended to as an end in itself. This choice is made even more dramatic because many theologians do find *an intimacy yet unnamed with God* in their time of study and reading. This intimacy needs to be named, embraced, and deepened. Naming this intimacy opens the well of grace that is our personal call to be a theologian. For many of us there is an unspoken depth to our chosen profession: "The reason I love theology is that I meet God and His love within study. Study is really 'our time.'" If this reality is appropriated, then we can enter a life of secured interiority, knowing within our mind not only levels of professional competency but also communion and consolation from God as well. This aspect of the call to be a theologian, shared with seminarians will transform academic formation.

It seems that Newman might have struggled with this tension between time for study and time for explicit prayer.

He longed for an integration of intellect and devotion, as he strove to cultivate what he called the "practice of the saintly intellect."[14] This term captures the true work of theology: to have the intellect energized in the face of mystery so that it may come to express this same mystery as fully as possible. As we pray together around our mission as theologians, our minds will become more concentrated in the heart.

Meditation

In subscribing to such a prayer commitment with colleagues, theologians are entering a familiar struggle in the academy: Do I ever, or even regularly, refuse to enter explicit prayer and choose instead the duties that engage me in theological research?

Praying Alone

As we prepare for class or theological research, our best intentions are always to avoid letting the rush of the seminary day define our work. Instead, we want Christ and His mission to orient us. In this valley of tears, where our nature is wounded by sin, such goals will be met as best we can within our limited resources. Still, we draw our healing power from the resurrected Christ and His sharing the Holy Spirit with us, and so we always begin again, and we hope anew that our prayer lives as theologians can and will deepen over the years. To this end we need to intentionally specify and keep our personal commitment to prayer. We urge our seminarians to do the same. We urge such consistency in prayer for the seminarian quite often out of an intense and painful consciousness that our own prayer life is a struggle, much like Cardinal Newman's candid comment: "Often I find it difficult to even say my prayers."

Geography can be important to maintaining a personal prayer life. Note your daily route around the seminary. Where do you gravitate first upon arrival in the morning? The chapel? The desk? The library? The faculty room to read the morning newspaper? The refectory? Most morning routines are just that—routines—rather thoughtless, even random, paths that we walk to achieve some consoling end before the "work" begins. Does this morning routine facilitate prayer? More specifically, does our morning routine facilitate prayer for us *as theologians*? Do we need to suffer a new beginning or ending to our day? Do we need to find a new way to enter our theological study or class preparation, a way more hospitable to prayer? Are there ways that faculty meetings and committee meetings can become more soaked in prayer? Our commitment to personal prayer has public ramifications, since by way of prayer we are becoming different men and women. Do we allow our personal prayer and its effects on our character to affect the structure of our seminary day?

Each theologian must discern what changes need to be made to his or her personal *horarium*. Thus, the practice of spiritual direction is crucial. It is not rare to find priest theologians giving spiritual direction to seminarians while their own need for direction lies dormant. Spiritual direction is essential for the spiritual growth of all theologians on the faculty.

As we continue to develop our personal prayer time, we endeavor to listen to our interior "guest" at the deepest level possible when studying, writing a theological essay, or preparing class content. Of course we must pay attention to our arguments and other theological interlocutors, but we also need to descend to the level of divine communion in our work. If we allow these depths to attract us, over time we will be gifted with a secured interiority, a heart centered upon the indwelling Holy Spirit. If priestly formation is to reach its unique configuration as personal, intellectual, and spiritual transformation in the service of eliciting and sustaining pastoral desire in the seminarian, then the theologian must personally "put out into the deep" (Lk. 5:4) of worship.

Notes

1 "After breakfast, John Paul II would move into his study.... Even the time he set aside for study was peppered with prayers, with short bursts of prayer. So it was as if he never stopped praying throughout the day. It wasn't a rare occurrence for one of his secretaries to look for him and find him prostrate on the floor of the chapel, completely immersed in prayer." Stanislaw Cardinal Dziwisz, *A Life with Karol* (New York: Doubleday, 2008), 86.

2 See A. J. Conyers, *Listening Heart: Vocation and the Crisis of Modern Culture* (Texas: Spence, 2006), 154ff.

3 As quoted in James McCaffrey, *The Fire of Love: Praying with St. Therese* (Norwich: Canterbury Press, 1998), 82. This book is an insightful introduction into Therese's prayer life.

4 Second Vatican Council, *Gaudium et Spes* 43, 1965.

5 Pope John Paul II, *Ex Corde Ecclesiae* 16, 1990.

6 Corbon, *The Wellspring of Worship*, 43.

7 Conyers, *Listening Heart*, 67.

8 Corbon, *The Wellspring of Worship*, 106.

9 Romano Guardini, *Learning the Virtues That Lead You to God* (Manchester: Sophia, 1987), 184.

10 Ibid., 181.

11 Corbon, *The Wellspring of Worship*, 138.

12 "Our worship is a deep exercise of our spirits before the Lord, which doth not consist in an exercising of the natural part or natural mind, either to hear or speak words, or in praying according to what we, of ourselves, can apprehend or comprehend concerning our needs; but we wait, in silence of the fleshly part, to hear with the new ear, what God shall please to speak inwardly in our own hearts; or outwardly through others, who speak with the new tongue, which he unlooseth, and teacheth to speak; and we pray in the Spirit, and with the new understanding, as God pleaseth to quicken, draw forth, and open our hearts towards himself. Thus our minds being gathered into the measure, or gift of grace, which is by Jesus Christ; here we appear before our God, and here our God, and his Christ, is witnessed in the midst of us." Isaac Penington, *God's Teachings and Christ's Law*, "A Few Words Concerning the Worship which our God Hath Taught Us," Part XIII (1671), accessed online at www.qhpress.org/texts/penington/teaching.html.

13 John Henry Newman, *Meditations and Devotions* (London: Burns and Oates, 1964), 26-27.

14 See Terrence Merrigan, *Clear Heads and Holy Hearts: The Religious and Theological Ideals of John Henry Newman* (Louvain: Peeters Press, 1991), 254.

Chapter Six

Priestly Mission: Theology Ordered to Pastoral Charity

I n this final chapter I will contextualize our vocation as seminary theologians within a vision of
the kind of priests we want to form, and beyond
that the kind of laity we hope to see formed by the priests we
have instructed. I shift, then, from meditating upon the activities and identity of the seminary theologian *per se* (study,
teaching, worship) to sharing an image of what fidelity to
such an identity may yield in the life of the parish priest.
What vision of the priesthood should we hold in our hearts
so that our work remains vibrant and focused?

I will also present a vision of the relationship between
the priest's vocation and the vocation of the laity within
the secular culture. How does our vocation as contemplative theologians contribute to the ability of seminarians to

understand the magnitude of the lay vocation? How can a seminarian come to reverence the mutually interpenetrating gifts of priest and laity? This final chapter, then, is a sketch of the kind of priest we hope to form simply by being faithful to our vocations as contemplative theologians.

Seminary Formation and Priestly Life: Two Spiritual Seasons

Seminarians

As noted formerly, the revised version of the *Program of Priestly Formation* states: "Since spiritual formation is the core that unifies the life of the priest, it stands at the heart of seminary life and is the center around which all other aspects are integrated."[1] This truth comes to the seminary as both a healing and challenging word. It is *healing* because it brings both formators and seminarians to the *very source of vocation: communion with Christ and His Church.* In so doing, the seminarian's heart becomes open to the healing that Christ always brings: the healing of sinfulness in moral conversion, the healing of ideology and error in intellectual conversion, and finally, the healing of memories and inordinate emotional attachments in affective conversion. The seminary seeks to prepare, form, and heal all of its students so they can stand before parishioners as true leaders of the Spirit-imbued interior life, the fountain of all pastoral charity.

The message of the revised *Program of Priestly Formation* is *challenging* because it requires courage to look within and encounter the truth about ourselves and Christ through a lively and sustained prayer life. It is much easier to fashion a seminary program around the competencies needed for academic achievement, pastoral presence, and human development than to regularly stand *vulnerable before the Lord* in all facets of seminary formation. This does not imply that accomplishing an intellectual achievement or weathering a difficult psychological suffering is without labor. Even this hard work, however, can be used to escape from the penetrating gaze of Christ's invitation to come and follow Him. This truth-bearing, albeit loving, gaze is what some often strive to avoid in the routine busyness of the seminary *horarium*. If spirituality is to be the core of priestly formation, it is necessary to promote the disposition to encounter Christ interiorly in the midst of ordinary duties. Living in the seminary community is an ever-deepening challenge to become *vulnerable to Christ* in all things, even as He enables such vulnerability and invites us to levels of spiritual intimacy not previously experienced.

Seminary Formators

Spiritual directors and seminary theologians need to think in new ways about their relationship. This collaboration must develop in the manner that the relationship between pastoral formation and academics has developed, or how the relationships have progressed among faculty, the personal formation team, and the staff psychologist at some seminaries. More often, however, the spiritual director, and therefore spirituality, appears to be consistently isolated in the minds of faculty. Some of this separation stems from the traditional nature of spiritual direction, which defines itself as being located only in the internal forum. If we equate the spiritual lives of the seminarians to spiritual direction, we run the risk of reducing spirituality to the private conversation of the internal forum. We must find ways to encourage the theological faculty to enter into explicit dialogue with seminary spiritual directors in order to explore ways to bring spirituality out into the public forum.

The spiritual life for the diocesan priest can be described as a life of "intimate and unceasing union with God the Father through his Son, Jesus Christ, in the Holy Spirit.... Those who aspire to be sent on mission ... must first acquire the listening and learning heart of disciples."[2] Further specified, priestly spirituality draws a man "into the priestly, self-sacrificial path of Jesus.... [He gives] his life as a ransom for the many. He is the Good Shepherd who lays down His life.... He is the bridegroom who loves his bride, the Church, 'and handed himself over for her.'"[3] All of these identities attempt to capture the unity between the mission of Christ and the men He calls to further this mission in the priesthood. As Christ identified Himself with the poor *in their need,* He identifies Himself with the priest's healing action of *spousal love and self-offering service.* Thus Christ is all in all—He is the servant and the served, the bridegroom and the bride. The seminary, a community wherein spirituality integrates all essential formational realities, is the place where an emotionally healthy man[4] wills to be deeply affected by this integration; it is for him that such a school is ordered.

This healing is not simply for him as an end, however, but for him in his ministry. The integrating power of spirituality matures him as a man, attracts him as a "husband," and then establishes him as a "father," with each step deepening his ever-developing capacity to give himself away to the Bride of Christ without undue thought of self.[5] Like all husbands, however, his primary good *is the good of his Bride*. If the seminarian has discerned his vocation correctly, such self-giving is the only route to walk that promises happiness. Seminary theologians who welcome spirituality as the integrating core of their mission will present to seminarians a way to become such spiritual husbands.

The faculty does this by structuring the day in a way that allows the seminarian to welcome the Bridegroom. The Bridegroom will school the seminarians in how to espouse the Church, an espousal that attains full potency after ordination. Christ sacramentally extends His salvific acts in time by way of the man who has consented to become both spouse and father, the diocesan priest. In and through academics, prayer, worship, counseling, and pastoral work, Christ fills the seminarian's heart with a communion that heals sin and error while gifting him with a wisdom received according to his developmental capacities. To think that such a public ordering is inappropriate for a seminary—mistakenly believing that spirituality is essentially a private matter between a seminarian and his spiritual director—is to identify a prime weakness in faculty consciousness to date.

Spirituality and Ministry Formation

Spirituality will never be the integrating core of seminary life if the faculty does not aid seminarians in identifying the many interior movements and external manifestations of everyday grace. Failure to develop this skill of discernment within all seminarians is to send them out to the parish ill-equipped to assist the laity in naming their own experiences of grace and awakening their receptivity to being taken up in the Paschal Mystery—the birthplace, in faith, of all of life's meaning.

Promoting spirituality as the core of priestly formation and life may leave some faculty wondering whether such an interpretation is a shift from the focus upon pastoral charity that defined priestly identity at the time of the Second Vatican Council.

> In the world of today, when people are so burdened with duties and their problems, which oftentimes have to be solved with great haste, and range through so many fields, there is considerable danger of dissipating their energy. Priests, too, involved and constrained by so many obligations of their office, certainly have reason to wonder how they can coordinate and balance their interior life with feverish outward activity....
>
> ... Priests, then, can achieve this coordination and unity of life by joining themselves with Christ to acknowledge the will of the Father. For them this means a complete gift of themselves to the flock committed to

them. Hence, *as they fulfill the role of the Good Shepherd, in the very exercise of their pastoral charity they will discover a bond of priestly perfection which draws their life and activity to unity and coordination.* This pastoral charity flows out in a very special way from the Eucharistic sacrifice. This stands as the root and center of the whole life of a priest. What takes place on the altar of sacrifice, the priestly heart must make his own. This cannot be done unless priests through prayer continue to penetrate more deeply into the mystery of Christ.[6]

Decontextualized, this could be misconstrued as "My ministry is my spirituality." The actions that incarnate pastoral charity may coordinate and unify priestly ministry, but that in itself does not exhaust the meaning of the text. The context of such unity and coordination is crucial to recall. All pastoral charity flows from participation in the Paschal Mystery of Christ. If there is no subjective communion with the Mystery, then priestly ministry might become "feverish." Rather than shifting the emphasis, the *Program of Priestly Formation* explicitly radicalized the teaching of the Second Vatican Council. In saying that pastoral charity unifies the life of the priest, the Council Fathers *rooted that charity in communion with Christ* and His mysteries upon the altar. The *Program of Priestly Formation* founds *pastoral charity upon a spiritual union with Christ's Mysteries*, thus protecting a rightful understanding of charity from descending into a "life of busy Church work." All true pastoral charity flows from an interior communion with God in the context of ecclesial orthodoxy. Communion with Jesus Christ, as fostered by an intense prayer life, is the essential source from which pastoral charity flows. This charity orders priestly character habitually toward serving the laity so that they, in turn, can transform the secular world for Christ.

Keeping spiritual formation at the center of seminary life, around which all other aspects of formation are integrated, helps to assure that seminarians suffer the death of their egos while concurrently welcoming communion with the Trinity. Forming men in these mysteries aids in reducing their risk of going through seminary for the wrong reasons, inappropriately attached to the lingering shadows of priestly life: social standing, privilege, entitlement, and "bachelor" independence. Without Christ transforming them from within by way of all four pillars of formation, a seminarian may be seduced to espouse the Church in spiritually and affectively immature ways. If this seduction is effective, he may use pastoral work for his own unhealthy ends. This transformation by Christ, however, is not magic; it must be noted that such a conversion is more likely to occur when Christ's wisdom and truth dwells within a faculty that has suffered its own conversion and healing.

The words of Pope John Paul II reveal how priestly spiritual formation relates to *the fruit* of such disciplined living, pastoral charity:

> Pastoral study and action direct one to an inner source, which the work of formation will take care to guard and make good use of: This is the ever-deeper communion with the pastoral charity of Jesus, which— just as it was

the principle and driving force of his salvific action—likewise, thanks to the outpouring of the Holy Spirit in the sacrament of orders, should constitute the principle and driving force of the priestly ministry. It is a question of a type of formation meant not only to ensure scientific, pastoral competence and practical skill, but also and especially a way of being in communion with the very sentiments and behavior of Christ the good shepherd: "Have this mind among yourselves, which is yours in Christ Jesus" (Phil. 2:5).[7]

There can be no separation or competing emphases between the realms of spiritual formation and pastoral charity according to this description, because pastoral charity flows from the Church's communion with Christ (spirituality). In fact, as John Paul II states, communion with Christ is communion *with his own pastoral charity*.[8] The pope further connects priestly spiritual formation with a sound devotion to the Sacred Heart of Christ. Entering into communion with the Heart of Christ is to enter that with which Christ communed: the Father's will.[9] Pope John Paul's advice is to carefully guard this interior source of formation; this core intimacy with Christ must be protected, because such intimacy is the personal life-blood of all priests. Without such communion with the pastoral charity of Christ, the priest simply ministers, with ever-growing faintness, from the resources of his own will.

John Paul II also illuminates the dynamic relationship between pastoral charity and spirituality, a relationship never to be separated:

This same pastoral charity is the dynamic inner principle capable of unifying the many different activities of the priest. In virtue of this pastoral charity *the essential and permanent demand for unity between the priest's interior life and all his external actions and the obligations of the ministry can be properly fulfilled*, a demand particularly urgent in a socio-cultural and ecclesial context strongly marked by complexity, fragmentation and dispersion. Only by directing every moment and every one of his acts toward the fundamental choice to "give his life for the flock" can the priest guarantee this unity which is vital and indispensable for his harmony and spiritual balance. The Council reminds us that "priests attain to the unity of their lives by uniting themselves with Christ whose food was to fulfill the will of him who sent him to do his work.... In this way, by assuming the role of the good shepherd they will find in the very exercise of pastoral charity the bond of priestly perfection which will unify their lives and activities."[10]

Meditation

How can we keep the beauty of pastoral charity that flows out of communion with Christ from simply becoming acts of kind regard toward others?

The basic realities of communion with Christ's Mysteries (an interior principle) and its fruit as service to the Bride of Christ in pastoral charity can never be separated. They do, however, have a constitutive order if maturity in priestly identity is to be reached. Priestly ministry flows from union with Christ, whether symbolized by the Eucharist or by liturgical and personal prayer. Ministry flows from and is secured by communion with Mystery since "holiness itself contributes very greatly to a fruitful fulfillment of the priestly ministry"[11]. A man's seminary years ought to be a time of cultivating a deep interiority, even while he is mentored in how the fruit of this interiority is manifested prudentially in public ministry.[12]

This communion with the pastoral charity of Christ is one that organically develops within the seminarian by his regular commitment to the sacramental life, personal prayer, scripture study, and service to those in need. The structure of the seminary can facilitate this ever-deepening communion, or it can hinder him in this intimacy. To assist the seminarian, the faculty ought to be porous to the presence of Christ on all levels. This can be symbolized by looking toward the domestic Church, wherein good parents, for example, will never block the coming of Christ into their own or their children's consciousness, but rather they strive to facilitate it. These parents will encourage the coming of Christ whether it is over the dinner table, during routine conversation, working together in the yard, in the midst of entertainment, or whenever appropriate. Similarly, all seminary faculty members ought to be "weak points" through which God can reach the seminarian, regardless of the theologian's specialty or field of competence.

If the structure of the seminary tolerates compart-
mentalization and leaves spiritual realities only to the set
times of public prayer and spiritual direction, the seminarian
will not gain the facility needed to find God in all things, nor
will he be an expert in supporting the laity as they enter their
own mission of finding God in all things secular. Spirituality holds a patina of privacy since it is synonymous in some
people's minds with a narrowed understanding of interiority. Interiority is not an end in itself. Analogically, a husband
seeks his wife for intimacy so that he may give himself to her
and she may give herself to him, but they do so as part of the
larger mission of constituting a very public reality, a family.
Their communion, analogous here to interiority, is entered
so that from such union life may flow: their own emotional
and spiritual life, as well as any new life in the conception
and birth of a child. Those who seek Christ within the heart,
and therefore commune with His own pastoral charity, do so
ultimately to give life to others through ministry. Anything
less for those pursuing priesthood is misguided. Interiority
does not have ego comfort as its goal.

Developing and Sustaining a Priestly Life: A Vision for the Seminary Theologian

Charity takes up residence in a priest's soul as a gift.
This charity is God revealing, sharing, and communicating
Himself in a continuing and eternal act of spousal care to-
ward humanity. This care reaches its ultimate self-gift in the

nakedness of Christ upon the cross—the marriage of the Lamb and the Bride (Rev. 19:7). This charity, living in the soul, is no different from the supernatural gift, the indwelling of God, that inhabited this man's soul at Baptism, Confirmation, and Eucharist. [13] It is the same charity, now *bearing the grace* of a call. This call summons him to come out from among the members of the Church and "be Christ" by serving "His Bride" as priest. The grace of ordination allows the charity that is in everyone's heart (love of God, love of neighbor) to be specifically the grace of being with Christ in His spousal love for the Church. This new ordering in the sacrament places the priest in relationship to the Body of Christ *as a whole*. He relates to all the members of the Body, sharing in the prophetic, kingly, and priestly ministry of Christ. The laity relate to the priest out of their own distinctive participation in these same Christological realities. The mode of existing in and among the members of the Church is always interrelationship.

The communion between this man, the God who calls him, and the laity constitutes a spirituality—the breath of life between them all—that binds the facets of priestly formation together. The goal of this communion is to form the contemplative heart of the husband-priest. This priest gazes upon the Body of Christ, the Church, the Bride, not with a sense of entitlement or "lust" (using the office of priest for his own end) but with an ever-growing pastoral desire, a desire born of this spiritual communion and finding its purpose and rest only in charitable service.

Charity is the Father's love in and through the love of Jesus (cf. Jn. 15:9). A man subjectively receiving this

184 *Resting on the Heart of Christ*

objective love of God accomplishes Jesus' most ardent desire for his priests: "Remain in my love" (Jn. 15:9). From this communion will flow the living water of pastoral ministry (Jn. 7:37ff). This ministry is first born in the heart of a praying priest, a priest who receives charity as his joy, as his point of intimacy with the Trinity, as God dwelling within him through the grace of Christ. The priest's intimacy with this indwelling Presence is the furnace that accomplishes his own purification. Charity, thus, makes him a son "responding to the love of Him 'who first loved us.'"[14] No one has a right to communion with God except the Son and anyone to whom the Son wishes to share His birthright (Mt. 11:27). All need to be purified; such a process begins at Baptism, but the priest is configured to the Son in a priestly way, in a way that gifts him with the call to house the *actions of Christ* as the priest's *way* of being embodied, his way alone.

The priest is irreplaceable, just as one's own father is irreplaceable. Others may do similar actions, but none can be present in certain actions in the way that only "my" father and only "our" priest can. Numerous stories circulate when a friendly neighbor or care-giver tries to fill the shoes of an absent or deceased dad and is met with the uncomfortable words of an adopted, foster, or orphaned child saying, "Are you trying to be my dad? No one can be my dad." Certain presences—and only those presences—can mediate particular actions to the point of bearing their full fruit. A prayerful man from the parish congregation can lead intercessory prayers, share scripture, and catechize, but if he dons an alb and stole, the Church would say, "Are you trying to be our pastor, our spiritual father? No one can replace our priest."

The whole Bride is promised communion with the Trinity by the grace of Christ's mission, but only the priest shares in that mission directly. At his ordination the priest is made vulnerable to Christ's desire to *live His saving mysteries over again* in him, and so he is entrusted with a priestly vocation. The personal happiness of the priest and part of the effectiveness of his ministry depends upon the priest's capacity to *entrust himself* to Christ, to seek and receive abiding communion with Him.[15] *Interiority*, then, conditions and constitutes pastoral charity.

Without a lively interior life of communion with Christ, the priest loses touch with his unique character as one sent from Christ through the bishop to sacramentally minister a divine and saving love to Christ's Bride. He loses touch with the uniqueness of his call from Christ to live the same kind of embodied life as did Christ: chaste, celibate, and self-giving. A priest knows the fullness of his call precisely from an interior communion giving rise to pastoral desire sated in ministry. He certainly ministers grace in the sacraments *objectively*, but Christ wants the man himself to have life and life abundantly, not simply mediate life to the people he serves (Jn. 10:10).

St. Therese's reflection on the gift of her communion with Christ, and how it led to her service of others and to her deep interior peace, captures this priestly dynamic:

> In one instant Jesus accomplished what I had been unable to do for several years, having been content on my part, with my good will, which had never been wanting.... Just like the Apostles, I was able to say, "Lord I have

fished all night and taken nothing." Being
more merciful towards me than He was towards His disciples, Jesus Himself took hold
of the net, cast it out and drew it in filled
with fishes. He made me a fisher of souls.... I
felt a great desire to labor for the conversion
of sinners.... In a word, I felt charity enter my
heart, the need to forget myself that I might
please others, and from that time I have
been happy."[16]

We can pray for a gift. Jesus Himself is *the* answered prayer
of all time. He came as gift in response to a cry of loneliness,
meaninglessness, and the lost wanderings of sinners. The
priest must cry out and receive the gift of charity that has entered his soul. This appropriation of the Divine indwelling,
of communion with the Holy Spirit, is the personal wellspring of his ministry. Such communion will sustain him as
he enters the lives of his parishioners and their experiences
of joy, boredom, and the ever-present summons of death and
suffering. The Mystery of God within the priest animates
such interior charity, sustaining him even when he is not
aware of it. For the priest, the love of Christ compels him
(2 Cor. 5:14). The life of pastoral charity is irresistible to the
priest who invites Christ to define his interiority and fashion
his affections and conscience according to the mysteries of
salvation. Pope Benedict XVI wrote:

> This is the central task of the priest: to bring
> God to men and women. Of course, he can
> only do this if he himself comes from God, if
> he lives *with* and *by* God....

...This theocentricity of the priestly existence is truly necessary in our entirely function-oriented world in which everything is based on calculable and ascertainable performance. The priest must truly know God from within and thus bring him to men and women: this is the prime service that contemporary humanity needs. If this centrality of God in a priest's life is lost, little by little the zeal in his actions is lost. In an excess of external things the centre that gives meaning to all things and leads them back to unity is missing.[17]

Priesthood and Lay Life: Two Vocations Bearing Mutually Interpenetrating Gifts

Addressing the formation of the seminarian and the spiritual life of the priest necessarily points to the Church they serve, the object of their ministry and sacrifice, especially the lives of parishioners. A seminary faculty will never be faithful to its mission unless it is focused on forming priests who love and draw their lives from Christ, inviting the seminarians into the depths and allowing the Lord to teach them how to live within such depths. Living within these depths is not simply for the priest; rather, it is the very gift he gives to the laity. The faculty, then, must also be fascinated with lay holiness. The paradox of the priest is that the life God called him away from—wife and children—must become the life that rivets his imagination and love. When Christ calls a man away from marriage, He does so only so that he is free in Christ to serve all marriages and families. Christ *never asks priests not to be husbands and fathers.* Instead He asks them to husband in the same embodied way that He does: in a life of chaste celibacy. The privilege of this invitation, to be embodied in the same way as Christ, is an endless source of humility for the priest. "Why was I called to husband in this way of deep affinity with Christ, ordered toward that which Christ loves above all, His Bride, the Church?"

Meditation

When I teach, how do I assist the seminarian in keeping his spousal identity before him in a concrete way so he can integrate it within his studies?

Any man who loves the *idea* of priesthood (clericalism) more than his service to the laity ought not to be a priest. Emotionally and spiritually healthy priests always desire to be *with* and *for* "their people." This is true, maybe especially true, even if a priest is carrying out a necessary service for the good of the diocese or universal Church that draws him away from parish work. Any husband serving his country in the military or traveling for business longs to be with his bride. Even as he knows that in some way his work is *for* his bride, he longs to be *with* her. The priest longs for his parish, for his people, and to enact the spiritual help he can bring to them. Christ has called him to be a priest so that he may minister Christ to the laity, and the seminary faculty needs to reverence this call by introducing the seminarian to a sustained treatment of the theology and spirituality of the lay vocation.

These two vocations, priest and lay, are never to be separated or set against each other in any way. Like any husband and wife, having one without the other simply makes the vocation incomprehensible. The bridegroom brings out and supports what the bride is meant to become, and the bride brings out and supports what the bridegroom is meant to become. Though the lay vocation and the priestly vocation are held in *equal* esteem at the level of the *human dignity of each individual who receives these callings*, a *difference* remains that must be celebrated and maintained between both vocations.[18] Vocations are incommutable. The laity have an independence from the clergy in many areas of Church life by virtue of their baptism,[19] but it is clear that the laity receive their *identity* from the sacraments, whose ordinary ministers are priests.[20]

These words cited by John Paul II make it clear that the priest is to initiate the laity into the Mysteries of Christ:

> Spiritual formation ... should be conducted in such a way that the students may learn to live in intimate and unceasing union with God the Father through his Son Jesus Christ, in the Holy Spirit. Those who are to take on the likeness of Christ the priest by sacred ordination should form the habit of drawing close to him as friends in every detail of their lives. They should live his paschal mystery in such

a way that they will know how to initiate into
it the people committed to their charge.[21]

An objective reality—specifically the sacramental
life—is present in the ministry of the priest, the salvific presence of the Christ not encountered or received in any other
form of spiritual regimen. This sacramental life, ministered by
priests, is the foundation of all Christian reality, prayer, and
service. The laity are initiated into these mysteries through
the priesthood. This initiation occurs objectively when sacraments are celebrated by any priest, but the priest's love for
the mystery and his ongoing conversion carry a charism, a
grace, to the people receiving the sacraments. Analogically, a
man can simply fulfill a debt to another, or he can give more
than what is owed by sharing a personal presence with the
payee, making the exchange human. Rather than minimally
fulfilling the requirements of justice the exchange becomes
an act of grace.

The spirituality of the priesthood beckons the man
to enter the depths of the mystery he lives: "How do I more
fully embody the presence of Christ in His ministry—not
only for my parishioners but also for the sake of my own happiness?" Christ does not simply want his people to receive
salvation and holiness sacramentally but to receive it at the
hands of a *holy priest*. Here it is clear that the priest goes deep
so he can go broad. The priest longs to share the Mysteries of
Christ with his people—a people living a life marked by a
secular character, witnessing to the culture the transforming
power of being defined by the Paschal Mystery. This holy lay
life is made available through Christ's own words and actions
by way of a sacramental priesthood.

The relationship between the priest who sacramentally mediates Christ and desires interior communion with Him and the laity's mission to go and transform culture is necessarily linked by Christ in the Eucharist. For the adult lay person, the dismissal at the conclusion of the Eucharist is truly a sending by Christ to the fields of harvest found in the secular world.[22] Upon their return to the Eucharist the following week, the laity offer the fruit of their public lives as an oblation to the Father through Christ. Witnessing this fruit at the liturgy is key to the celibate priest's subjective motivation to continue welcoming the Mystery of Christ at ever-deepening mystical levels.[23] As a spouse contemplates the spiritual and moral growth of his or her beloved since marriage, finding a place to invest the meaning and purpose of nuptial self-giving, so the priest looks to the converted lives of the laity, and even deeper to the effects these lives have upon the transformation of culture, to invest his life's purpose. Contemplating such a transformation of the Bride of Christ, the priest finds the meaning of his life's self-offering.

This communion between the priestly and lay vocations may not always be self-evident. If such a rift is to be bridged, seminary faculty must dedicate themselves to facilitating the spiritual formation of the seminarian in ways that will enable him to unleash within his future congregation a *love for lay life*, a life that can only be sustained by an impassioned and intentional love for the Eucharistic mystery. After decades of listening to many voices in the Church flatten the distinction between priest and laity, the Church may be no closer to healing the separation bemoaned by the Council Fathers forty years ago: "One of the gravest errors of our time is the dichotomy between the faith which many profess and the practice of their daily lives."[24]

The flattening of the distinction between the sacred and the profane was intended to speed the arrival of a just world and Church. Christ's mission was not to be served by hierarchical division but only by the universal triumph of baptismal identity; the egalitarian approach to lay-clergy relations was supposed to open up many possibilities for ecclesial and social renewal. In the end, however, the Church has a spiritual or religious mission.[25] Emphasizing a politicized mission weakened this foundation. For the spiritual mission to go forward, the distinct yet mutually-interpenetrating relationships of the priestly life and the lay mission to the secular world must be cultivated, not crushed. Pope John Paul II noted in his encyclical *Christifideles Laici*:

> The ordained ministries ... express and realize a participation in the priesthood of Jesus Christ that is different, not simply in degree but in essence, from the participation given to all the lay faithful through Baptism and Confirmation. On the other hand, the ministerial priesthood ... is ordered toward the priesthood of all the faithful.[26]

Meditation

How might I more explicitly connect the gift of priesthood to the vocation of the laity in the minds of my students?

In this relationship, the priestly vocation stands as a gift to the laity, who are sustained by the Mystery of Christ at the Eucharist.[27] The priesthood, without which no Eucharist can be celebrated, is given to the Church by Christ so that His salvation and grace can continue in time and space. Lay persons offer their lives to Christ in the Eucharist and bring the fruit of their witness in secular society to the Eucharist so that it may be given to the Lord as He continues to bless lay efforts to transform culture in His name. In this fruitfulness, the laity is a gift to the priesthood, as a priest sees in the laity's public witness, even to the point of sacrifice, the fruit of the Spirit that flows through his own sacramental ministry.

Without such lay witness in the secular world, priests might be tempted to think their ministry lacks spiritual power, purpose, and fecundity. With a vigorous lay witness in the secular world, the priest can contemplate his sacrifice of wife and family as a valued sign of Christ's own way of embodiment. In the priest's response to the call of Christ to live His form of embodiment over again, we find the virtue of Christ's own spousal love enlivening His Bride, the Church. The Church responds by meeting the gift of Christ's own life with their own lives, offered as spiritual worship (Rom 12:1-2) in the midst of secular commitments. Without the sacraments the laity are famished, and their minds become "worldly" rather than rightfully secular (i.e., *distinct* from God/hierarchy, not *separate* from God/hierarchy). At the Eucharist, the vocation of the laity and the vocation of the priest have their deepest communion and exist together *in Christ* so that His salvific action may continue in the priest's ministry, ultimately becoming embedded in the culture by the witness and action of the laity. Without the distinct vocations of clergy and laity, the presence of Christ would not have its endless font of renewal in the Eucharist; nor would the presence of Christ course from the Eucharist through the life of His members to assist the poor hidden in places that only the laity reach day in and day out. Together the priesthood and the laity give hope that Christ will remain always, even until the "end of the age" (Mt 28:20). The secular character of the laity serves and the spirituality of the priesthood gives witness to this Christic end.

Notes

1 *PPF* 115.

2 Ibid., 107.

3 Ibid., 109.

4 "Seminarians in need of long term therapy should avail themselves of such assistance before entering seminary, or should leave the program until therapy has been completed. If such a departure is indicated there should be no expectation of automatic re-admission" (*PPF* 105).

5 I use the word "husband" because it is the nature of the man to give himself to the bride (see *PDV* 23). This spousal giving needs to be emphasized in light of the Vatican's document on homosexuality and seminary formation (Congregation for Catholic Education, *Instruction Concerning the Criteria for the Discernment of Vocations*, 2005). The priest gives himself to serve the Bride of Christ. The use of the word "husband" fires the imagination for the heterosexual seminarian that he is still called to give himself in a way that a husband wants to, fully. Like all husbands and fathers, the priest is a source of life, albeit spiritual life alone. Seminarians do not have to "give up a masculine identity," since priesthood is a response to Christ calling them to husband His Church. This husbanding is unique. Christ wants the priest to protect and serve the one He gave His life up for, His Bride. It is Christ's Bride that is entrusted to the husband-priest, not his own. Priesthood extends the presence of Christ's own spousal love in time so that Christ can sacramentally continue His care for His Bride, the Church. The discernment question for all seminarians is: Is your way of being a husband to share in Christ's own priesthood as embodied in chaste celibacy, or does it lie in sacramental marriage?

6 Vatican Council II, *Presbyterorum Ordinis* 14; italics added.

7 Pope John Paul II, *PDV* 57. See also 23: "The internal principle, the force which animates and guides the spiritual life of the priest inasmuch as he is configured to Christ the head and shepherd, is pastoral charity, as a participation in Jesus Christ's own pastoral charity, a gift freely bestowed by the Holy Spirit and likewise a task and a call which demand a free and committed response on the part of the priest.

The essential content of this pastoral charity is the gift of self, the total gift of self to the Church, following the example of Christ. 'Pastoral charity is the virtue by which we imitate Christ in his self-giving and service. It is not just what we do, but our gift of self, which manifests Christ's love for his flock. Pastoral charity determines our way of thinking and acting, our way of relating to people. It makes special demands on us.'

The gift of self, which is the source and synthesis of pastoral charity, is directed toward the Church. This was true of Christ who 'loved the Church and gave himself up for her' (Eph. 5:25), and the same must be true for the priest. With pastoral charity, which distinguishes the exercise of the priestly ministry as an *amoris officium*, 'the priest, who welcomes the call to ministry, is in a position to make this a loving choice, as a result of which the Church and souls become his first interest, and with this concrete spirituality he becomes capable of loving the universal Church and that part of it entrusted to him with the deep love of a husband for his wife.' The gift of self has no limits, marked as it is by the same apostolic and missionary zeal of Christ, the good shepherd, who said: 'And I have other sheep, that are not of this fold; I must bring them also, and they will heed my voice. So there shall be one flock, one shepherd' (Jn. 10:16)."

8 Ibid., 23.

9 Ibid., 49.

10 Ibid., 23, quoting *Presbyterorum Ordinis* 14.

11 Ibid., 24.

12 A seminarian wanting to know and be known by Christ never inhibits pastoral charity unless there is some affective or psychological malady; even then Christ sometimes uses those who are close to Him and His mysteries, as is evident in some saints who were not necessarily free from all emotional or psychological illness. The Church, however, must guard the priesthood by ordaining only healthy men; if God wishes to infuse His grace in persons with emotional or psychological deficits, that, of course, is up to Him. The astute seminary faculty will frequently be able to detect a man using the language of piety, devotion, and interiority as a way to hide from truths that are too personally painful for him to bear. This abuse of piety by some seminarians can make certain faculty cynical about spirituality. A mature faculty is able to be fair and not deny to the majority of seminarians a lively, devotional commitment to Christ within an affectively-imbued intellect, simply because of the abuse of the some students.

13 CCC 1266.

14 Ibid., 1828; 1 Jn. 4:19.

15 *PDV* 18.

16 Quoted in Francois Jamart, *Complete Spiritual Doctrine of St. Therese of Lisieux* (New York: Alba House, 2001), 165.

17 Pope Benedict XVI, "Address to the Roman Curia," December 22, 2006.

18 *Code of Canon Law* (Annapolis Junction: Canon Law Society of America, 1999), canon 208.

19 See canons 204-231.

20 See Pontifical Council for Justice and Peace, *The Compendium of the Social Doctrine of the Church* (Washington, DC: USCCB Publishing, 2005), 542.

21 *PDV* 45, quoting *Optatam Totius* 8.

22 The dismissal rite may be reconstructed to highlight this "sending" more explicitly (Pope Benedict XVI, *Sacramentum Caritatis* 51, 2007).

23 For the married clergy of the Eastern rite churches and those Roman priests who minister by way of the Pastoral Provision, these analogies can be relevant by sublating their own marriages into the marriage of Christ to the Church. In so doing, the married priest, who at times may feel that he has the burden of two full-time vocations, can gain wisdom from the normative teaching on celibacy in the Church, but also lend his voice of support to celibate priests in assisting them to see where a theology and spirituality of sacramental marriage helpfully informs the spiritual marriage of the priest and Christ's Church.

24 *GS* 43.

25 *GS* 42.

26 Pope John Paul II, *Christifideles Laici* 22, 1988.

27 Ibid., 14.

Conclusion

The unspoken desire of most priests is to have their sacrifice of wife and family affirmed in the laity's courage to transform culture in the name of Christ. Of course lay persons desire that their priest gift them with inspiration as well—lives lived *in persona Christi capitis*, not simply lives reflecting the choices of pragmatic bachelors. The parish stands as the place of mutual service between the two vocations, but it is also the place of challenge and, when fidelity leads to suffering, the place of consolation. In this way both vocations hint at the coming eschaton, wherein the sufferings of this world will weigh little in light of the healing brought about by fidelity to the vocation God has asked each to carry. Without each working out their respective witnesses in the Spirit, the relationship between the two vocations can become competitive, puny, and even mutually dismissive. All marriages can descend to these wretched dregs, even after having begun at great heights of hope.

The culmination of the work accomplished by the Spirit in cooperation with both vocations is to give the world a vision that sees the values of this age as relative. This passing age can never be the heart within which rest is found. Ecclesially these mutually-interpenetrating calls meet in the aisle of the Church each Sunday when the priest welcomes the overpowering life of Christ into the Church and the laity in turn bring to the Father, and secondarily the priest, the fruits of such unleashed power in their own lives: the bread and wine of a pro-life, charitable, hospitable, monogamous, just, and holy culture. In this exchange of gifts, the whole of life makes sense. In turn, the levels of interior peace and happiness within both vocations, lay and clerical, regain their depths because the meanings of both vocations are placed within Christ's Mysteries, and both draw their power and meaning from the same source of life: "This is my body given for you" (cf. Lk. 22:19).

In some parts of the world there is a dearth of priests. This crisis is brought about by a deeper vocation crisis: a dearth of laity who truly embrace their call to transform the culture for Christ. As the laity takes its call with utmost seriousness, a plethora of future priests will come from their ranks, because the eyes of these men will open and the sacrifice of family life will become meaningful. In viewing the power of the laity to transform culture according to the virtues of Christ and the teachings of His apostles, many young men will contemplate this truth and seek ordination: "If the Eucharist can transform men and women into such brave, just, and self-forgetting citizens, then I can sacrifice my desire to be husband and father in order to husband and father the

Church into an even deeper appropriation of what Christ means to do for them, with them, and through them." Truly, "deep calls to deep" (Ps. 42:8).

The priest is called to a real and sustained life of interiority. He is summoned to become a master of prayer, an expert—both intellectually and affectively—in the truth and power of the Paschal Mystery. From this interiority he will preach, teach, and serve the laity, as they in turn welcome Christ at the hands of the priest, allowing Him to claim their hearts. Then, from within the hearts of the laity, Christ will reach out to the world and offer to it the same Mystery that is forever taking place upon the altar of sacrifice and upon the altar of the laity's witness: the love of God crucified and raised from the dead.

For our vocation as seminary theologians to reach its fullness, the spiritual mission of the priest must become the lens through which we plan, develop, and coordinate our approach to theology. Contextualized within an atmosphere of spirituality, an environment wherein communion with Christ gives rise to pastoral charity, seminary theology will find its depth and breadth. Concentrating our minds in this communion with Christ, we will articulate a vision of priesthood that becomes the seminarian's touchstone for the meaning of his own spiritual fatherhood. Seminary theology then will flow from spiritual communion with Christ, informed by the spiritual and moral needs of the laity, and ordered toward the mutually-interpenetrating holiness of priest and people.

How do we assist seminarians to appropriate *the Mystery of Christ's love and truth* in their study of theology?

How do we do this from within the very content of our classes and writings? With our *own personal spiritual conversion fueling our deepest interest in theology*, such questions may never be answered to the satisfaction of all, but they will assuredly never again be muted.

I began this book hoping to motivate seminary theologians to fully embrace the freedom that seminary affords them. It is a community that reverences both study and communion with Christ, in the context of serving the complete formation of future priests. Can we begin an era of teaching theology that draws its spirit from lovingly beholding the Beauty of Christ as He appears in Truth?

The academic model alone is not sufficient for seminary formation. The spiritual pillar must become the integrating core of seminary formation, because *only it has the strength to carry both the Mystery of God and the mystery of man*. Now, true integration around communion with Christ must occur in seminary so that a secured interiority characterizes the priest. The integration that he suffers within himself during formation can then become his compass when leading the parish to holiness. The seminary theologian opens the Paschal Mystery to future priests, intellectually. We are called to do so in such a way that the seminarian can receive his impending ordination not as an entitlement or as some reward for academic achievement. We are to open the Paschal Mystery in a way that evokes gratitude in a man as he contemplates and experiences the joy of receiving what God desires to give him as gift: his priesthood.

Appendix

A Seminarian's Lectio: Reading to Know and to Receive Divine Love

I n order to help seminarians receive our teaching in a more contemplative manner I have constructed an approach to study and classroom learning for them. To share these suggestions with them will help facilitate their reception of your own contemplative approach to teaching:

1. Approach the text that is assigned or the classroom notes to be reviewed in prayer. Ask the Spirit to guide you through your study and enlighten you as to concepts that quicken your

204   *Resting on the Heart of Christ*

affection for communion with God. No study will be completely irrelevant to you; it will serve the truth, serve the needs of your people, or deepen your own intimacy with Christ.

2. What does this text *say*? What does this text *say to me*? What does this text lead me to *say to God*? What do I detect *God is saying to me* through this text?

3. Remember you are receiving the text on two levels, discursive and contemplative. The first level is what the text says in itself ("Will this be on the test?"). The second level is what God is saying to you about your conversion journey. They have an interpenetrating, symbiotic relationship, not oppositional. Record both levels in your notebook. To keep academic notes distinct from personal insights it can be helpful to divide your notebook. Use one side of the book as a spiritual journal and the other side to record discursive notes for academic study. The "journal" side of your notebook does not have to be elaborate but simply provides a place for you to briefly record what is personally relevant to your spiritual life. After class or study, these records can then be prayed over and shared with your spiritual director.

4. Review both the contemplative and discursive sections of your notebook (computer) in your daily study. You will see in some cases that they reinforce each other, making learning easier

because the objective has become personally enlivening on the spiritual level, and your own spiritual life becomes better rooted in truth, history, sacrament, virtue, and Scripture.

5. Bring your contemplative insights before the Blessed Sacrament and let them rest within your heart as it communes with His Sacred Heart. Christ wants to deepen these insights in you, because He wants you to think out of what you love, and He wants you to love what is highest, Himself. The goal is to make such holy conversation habitual. This virtue will help you continue to study as a priest and continue to revere both intellectual competency and spiritual communion with God.

6. Embrace lifelong intellectual study. The Church wants priests to be intellectuals, but always in a way that leads you to God. Those who do not complete their study in this fashion can become arrogant, thinking their ego and its power fashioned all the knowledge that their minds contain.

7. This knowledge that leads to communion is not meant for you alone. The fruit of your study and the fruit of your communion with God that arises within study are meant to be given to the Church. It is to be shared freely, with little or no reference to the self. Whoever attempts to share the fruit of *lectio divina* by way of the ego robs it

of its power. In such cases the listener is not led to God but instead stumbles over the speaker's ego, never getting a chance to see the face of God emerge from truth and beauty.

8. Keep your reading broad and deep enough to encompass more than just popular or new books on spirituality. You do not want to spend your life getting more of what satisfies less. Rather, read substantive works again and again. Like Scripture, substantive and classic works in spirituality always yield more wisdom each time they are read. Draw your knowledge from these works, and encounter God in prayer while receiving the deep wisdom of such books. If an original thinker emerges in your time, you will hear about him or her; be a discerning reader. Look at well-written biographies of saints or intellectuals as well; they can help us ponder grace and the power of the Spirit in people's lives.

9. Go to confession frequently; sinful thinking patterns influenced by the seven deadly sins cramp your mind and limit the expansive field of your imagination, often leading to cynicism. The man with the pure mind is able to delight in thought and receive the most unthinkable callings, invitations, and consolations from God; whereas the man who thinks like a sinner is limited in his thought patterns, usually dull of vision, perhaps

dwelling in safety, casting aside ideals, especially the one he cannot fathom at all: holiness.

10. Encourage one another to practice holy study. Cultivate a depth of soul. Practice conversing about how study has led you to a deeper relationship with Christ. Do this for both personal and vocational reasons. There are few things more maddening than encountering a cleric who has no interest in holy things, who has no depth, no ability to spontaneously pray from his heart, to counsel from his love of God, or to teach from what he has suffered in study. Cultivate a depth of soul.

11. As you read, study, and attend classes in a contemplative manner, remember that your goal is to have such a listening stance alter your desires. Seek a real encounter with truth and with Him who is Truth. You want your study to change what you desire; you want your desires to fasten upon Him who beguiles you so that He becomes the focus of all your thinking and affection for all eternity. You want the Lord to teach you to love prayer, the communication that will occupy your mind for all eternity.

12. Interest in your *own* spiritual lives (i.e., obsessed with our progress) is not the point. Rather, you are called to be interested in those founts that *deliver life to you*, those founts that attract because of their power, refreshment, and purity: The

book of creation, the book of the cross, the book of scripture, and the book of the saints. If you let these sources feed your mind, then your mind will become concentrated in your heart, and all your thinking will be the fruit of your love for God. As a result, you will become a contemplative even in action.

About the Author

Deacon James Keating, PhD

James Keating is the Director of Theological Formation for The Institute for Priestly Formation at *Creighton
University* in Omaha, Nebraska. In 1993 Dr. James Keating
was appointed by the Papal Nuncio to be Associate Professor
of Moral and Spiritual Theology in the School of Theology
at the *Pontifical College Josephinum*, in Columbus, Ohio. He
served in this capacity for thirteen years until 2006, when he
joined the IPF staff. Deacon Keating received his doctorate
in Roman Catholic Theology from *Duquesne University*; his
master's degree in Religious Studies from *Fordham University*; and his bachelor's in Religious Studies from *Siena College*.
He served as Visiting Professor at the University of St. Mary
of the Lake (Mundelein Seminary/Liturgical Institute),
Chicago. Some of his more than seventy essays on Christian
ethics and spirituality have appeared in *Downside Review,
Modern Theology, Irish Theological Quarterly, Communio,
Linacre Quarterly, Studies in Spirituality, Milltown Studies,
New Blackfriars, Church, Religious Studies and Theology, Pro
Ecclesia, Logos, New Theology Review, Spiritual Life, Pastoral
Life, Origins, Pastoral Review, Chicago Studies, Envoy, Semi-
nary Journal,* and *The Priest.*

He is the co-author of the books: *Moral Formation
in the Parish* with Anthony Ciorra (Alba House, 1998); and
*Conscience and Prayer: The Spirit of Catholic Moral Theol-
ogy* (Liturgical Press/Michael Glazier, 2001); *The Way of
Mystery: Eucharist and Moral Living* (Paulist Press, 2006)

with Father Dennis Billy, C.Ss.R. Dr. Keating is the author of *Pure Heart, Clear Conscience: Catholic Moral Life* (Liguori Press, 2003); *Crossing the Desert: Moral Conversion and Lent* (Liguori Press, 2001), and *Listening for Truth: A Life of Prayer and Virtue* (Liguori Press, 2002). He has a forthcoming book entitled *A Deacon's Retreat* (Paulist Press, 2009).

Dr. Keating served as editor of the *Josephinum Journal of Theology* (1993-2006). He is editor of the books from Paulist Press entitled, *Spirituality and Moral Theology: Essays from a Pastoral Perspective* (2000); *Moral Theology: Fundamental Issues and New Directions* (2004); and *The Deacon Reader* (2006), which won first place in the Catholic Press Association Awards for 2006. He has a weekly radio program addressing topics in Catholic spirituality and morality heard on KVSS, Omaha, serves as the General Editor of IPF Publications, and is a deacon in the Archdiocese of Omaha. Married to Marianne, they have three sons, Kristoffer, Jonathan, and Liam, and a daughter, Ina Mairead.